WALK THIS WAY

WALK THIS WAY

FOOTWEAR FROM THE STUART WEITZMAN COLLECTION OF HISTORIC SHOES

New-York Historical Society
In association with
D Giles Limited, London

NEW-YORK
HISTORICAL
SOCIETY
MUSEUM & LIBRARY

Edward Maeder

With contributions by Stuart Weitzman and
Valerie Paley

Published on the occasion of the exhibition *Walk This Way: Footwear from the Stuart Weitzman Collection of Historic Shoes* on display at the New-York Historical Society Center for Women's History from April 20, 2018, through October 8, 2018

First published in 2018 by GILES
An imprint of D Giles Limited
4 Crescent Stables, 139 Upper Richmond Road,
London, SW15 2TN, UK
www.gilesltd.com

ISBN: 978-1-911282-14-3

For the New-York Historical Society:
Project Director: Valerie Paley, Director, Center for Women's History and Vice President and Chief Historian, New-York Historical Society
Consulting Curator: Edward Maeder
Curatorial Coordinator: Jeanne Gutierrez
Volume editor: Anne Hoy
Photography: Glenn Castellano

For D Giles Limited:
Copy-edited and proof-read by Jodi Simpson
Designed by Hoop Design
Produced by GILES, an imprint of D Giles Limited, London
Printed and bound in China

FRONT COVER Pointed-toe lace-up pumps, ca. 1964, Stuart Weitzman Collection, no. 269 (Fig. 142)
BACK COVER Peep-toe evening shoes, ca. 1935, Stuart Weitzman Collection, no. 3 (Fig. 84)
FRONTISPIECE Evening sandals, ca. 1948, Stuart Weitzman Collection, no. 5 (Fig. 102)
PAGES 4 AND 5 (FROM LEFT TO RIGHT)
Pumps, late 1920s, Stuart Weitzman Collection, no. 247 (Fig. 49)
Pumps, ca. 1920, Stuart Weitzman Collection, no. 61 (Fig. 46)
Pumps, late 1920s, Stuart Weitzman Collection, no. 43 (Fig. 61)

CONTENTS

FOREWORD

A bit over a year ago, David Redden, the storied former Sotheby's auctioneer, telephoned to suggest that I join him for lunch together with one of his clients. David promised the lunch would not be a waste of my time; still, he did not reveal his client's name, offering only a single hint. "Do you own any Stuart Weitzman shoes?" he asked. "Yes," I told him. "Good!" he rejoined, emphatically. "Wear them!"

I was thrilled to meet Stuart Weitzman, whose signature over-the-knee boots I had recently purchased and was happy to show off at the lunch. The footwear motivated a fascinating story from Stuart about his inspiration for the boots' unique design. Listening to Stuart speak, I realized that not only was he a wonderfully talented designer, but a great storyteller as well. My rapt attention must have encouraged him because I learned quite a lot about him over lunch—his father's shoe factory in Haverhill, Massachusetts, his early designs, his experience as a student at the Wharton School at the University of Pennsylvania, his idea for providing one-of-a-kind "million dollar" shoes to Oscar nominees. I also learned that Stuart was a collector of antique shoes.

As Stuart talked about his collection and the rationale for the shoes' evolving design—shoes to be worn in the privacy of a woman's home, boots that covered a part of a woman's leg that might immodestly be exposed when a woman climbed into a coach, shoes that American suffragists wore as they marched through city streets, "sexy" heels that corresponded to changing norms of female attractiveness—I began to see the possibility of an unexpected and visually thrilling exhibition to be housed in our new Joyce B. Cowin Women's History Gallery, a part of our brand new Center for Women's History, the first ever within the walls of a major museum. I asked Stuart whether he might be willing to lend the collection to us for a women's history exhibit. Much to my delight, he was enthusiastic about the idea.

Conversations following the lunch with my colleagues Valerie Paley, New-York Historical's Chief Historian and Director of the Center for Women's History, and Margi Hofer, New-York Historical's Museum Director, confirmed my sense that our institution could mount a "shoe" exhibition that would be consistent with our mission while delighting and surprising visitors. Margi identified a curator, Edward Maeder, who set himself the daunting task of identifying, conserving, and arranging the photographing of the collection. What a great privilege it is to work with such incredible historians and curators as these!

Stuart himself has been an extraordinary partner in both our exhibition and this accompanying book. Beyond his brilliance in the field of fashion, his wide-ranging interests and activities epitomize the creative mind. He has spent much of his time in Spain, so I will quote the Spanish artist Pablo Picasso, whose monumental painted stage curtain hangs in our museum, to underscore my point: "Others have seen what is and asked why. I have seen what could be and asked why not."

As always, I want to thank our generous Board of Trustees, who have supported all of our important work. Above all, I want to acknowledge the outstanding leadership of our Board Chair, Pam Schafler.

Louise Mirrer, Ph.D.
President and CEO
New-York Historical Society

STAND AND CONQUER
The Stuart Weitzman Collection of Historic Shoes

STUART WEITZMAN

[previous page]
Stuart Weitzman,
designer
Nudist sandal,
ca. 2013
Suede
Courtesy of Stuart
Weitzman

In 1961, I took a seat next to my father in his Haverhill, Massachusetts, factory. He wanted me to learn the art of his business: designing exceptional shoes for women. I was a sophomore at the University of Pennsylvania's Wharton School, and had grand plans about heading to Wall Street. The first time he showed me how to carve a heel, he changed my mind—and my life—forever.

My own personal history is reflected in this book in a few particular shoes. The Million dollar sandal, for example, altered the trajectory of my business in 2002, when it earned so much global recognition (Fig. 1). I designed the sandal to be irresistible to any red carpet interviewer, because attention then was not being paid to shoes at the Academy Awards. Commentators would ask stars about their dresses, their hair, their jewelry—I felt it was time to draw some attention to their footwear. Today, the question "Who are you wearing?" is one that can rightly be asked from head to toe.

The Nudist sandal (see p. 10) was, in a way, the result of an opposite approach. I was trying to create the "little black dress" of shoes: a simple, sexy staple that would work for any high-profile appearance. This shoe also represents the power of celebrities to shape popular culture. The Nudist, with its sky-high heel, appears to be impractical for anyone who has to stand longer than ten minutes. After extensive testing and engineering, however, we overcame its impracticality. Now, thanks to its constant presence on red carpets, it has become an essential accessory in countless closets.

The inspiration for the Highland boot began the evening I saw the film *Pretty Woman*, and realized the striking appeal of the thigh-high boot (Fig. 2). There had to be a way for anyone to feel at ease wearing a similar style in a traditional work environment (rather than the one Julia Roberts represented). I thought about this boot for awhile, working to get it just right. And once it came out, *People* magazine declared it "The Accessory of the Year."

The most successful shoe in my entire career was actually another boot: the 50/50 (Fig. 3). I created it twenty-five years ago, and it remains popular for the simplest of reasons: it's as versatile as any design could possibly be. It looks equally good on everyone, whether worn with shorts, jeans, skirts, or suits.

1
Stuart Weitzman,
designer
Million dollar sandal,
2002
Leather, diamonds
Courtesy of Stuart
Weitzman

2
Stuart Weitzman,
designer
Highland boot, ca. 2013
Suede
Courtesy of Stuart
Weitzman

3
Stuart Weitzman,
designer
50/50 boot, ca. 1992
Patent leather
Courtesy of Stuart
Weitzman

Without question, then, the designs I consider most basic to our brand's DNA are the ones chosen collectively by thousands of women: lawyers, doctors, teachers, artists, mothers, and daughters, who claim a favorite and loyally wear the soles out. I have been lucky enough to connect with many of them personally; there is nothing I love more than hearing about the wedding shoe that holds beautiful memories, the lucky pump that helped land a first job, or the stiletto that led to an especially memorable night out. (So, yes, if you ever see me walking by, please stop and share your favorites, too!)

Most of this book, though, is dedicated to a far longer and greater evolution. These extraordinary antique shoes, which span several centuries and countries, tell an almost infinite number of stories. Stories of conformity and independence, culture and class, politics and performance.

Throughout history, shoes have often served to represent a woman's social status. In many royal courts, for instance, extreme footwear proved one's wealth. If you could barely stand, you obviously didn't have to concern yourself with hard work. And the higher your heel, the farther away you were from the common ground. But even commoners used their accessories to flash their cash. The more embroidered detail on your fine leather boots, the more you must have paid to have them made. And, of course, a striking shoe can still make a social impact today, as designs are thoughtfully selected to express certain moods, desires, or objectives.

You may notice that many of the designs here look particularly uncomfortable. This might be a good place to acknowledge that the majority of women's shoes have been designed by men. And, yes, form has traditionally surpassed function in importance. Who first decided that women had to suffer for beauty? Probably someone who'd rather not take credit for an increasingly antiquated idea.

Just as I love experimenting with rare materials and unexpected constructions, I am naturally drawn to unusual shoes, like the ones in this exhibit and its catalogue. For me, there's often been an irony to their appeal. Consider the tiny silk slippers worn by women with bound feet (Fig. 4), or the stiff wooden platforms made for the implicit purpose of impeding movement (Fig. 5). Many of these designs, gorgeous as they are, have inspired me to rethink the notion that pain and fashion must be faithful partners.

4
China
Lotus shoes,
late 19th century
Silk embroidery on silk
with leather and cotton
Stuart Weitzman
Collection, no. 103

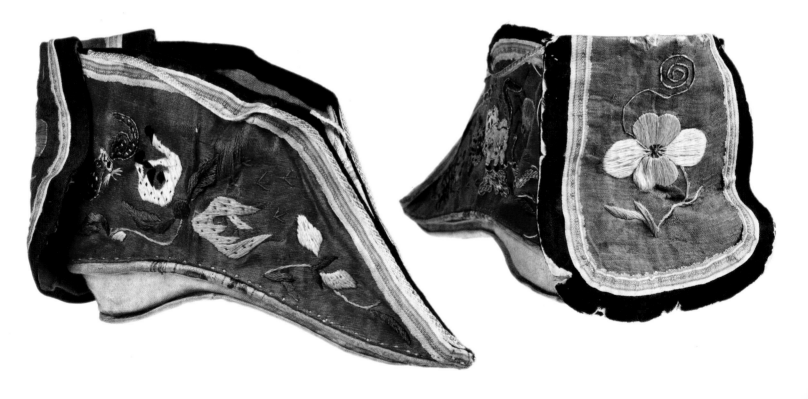

5
India
Toe-knob sandals,
19th century
Wood
Stuart Weitzman
Collection, no. 107

6
Sharon Von Senden
Jewels at Work,
undated
Stained glass, Swarovski
crystals, vintage stones
Photo by Lucas
Zarebinski
Collection of Jane
Gershon Weitzman

When more women entered the workforce in the early to mid-twentieth century, shoes *had* to become more comfortable. At the same time, handmade efforts began giving way to mass manufacturing. Many of the most beautiful shoes in these pages were crafted by small companies in tiny towns, servicing local communities. As businesses moved to larger centers of production, brand recognition became a crucial selling point. And a new level of professional competition required designers to become ever more creative if they wanted to make their mark.

As the women's movement of the 1960s and 70s pushed at the boundaries of identity, closets expanded further, to include espadrilles, sneakers, flip-flops, pumps at all heel heights, and boots of all types, from urban cowgirl to runway wannabe. By the twenty-first century, we've all become wise enough to realize that you're a lot more likely to look great if you feel great, too.

In another welcome shift, our industry began to see more and more women join the ranks of shoe designers. Roger Vivier, Salvatore Ferragamo, and my father—"Mr. Seymour"—were justly honored icons of another era. But Beth Levine, Margaret Clark, and Mabel Julianelli, among others—all overlooked for too long—deserve similar recognition. In fact, they forged the path for an industry in which women are now equally represented, and naturally they have put the art of comfort on the same plane as the art of design.

If you get as much enjoyment out of viewing these rare and beautiful antique shoes as I have had in accumulating them, the appreciation is due to my wife, Jane Gershon Weitzman. These shoes have been her gifts to me over fifty years, selected with a common purpose: to preserve and celebrate unusual and elegant detail and construction, and to provide an inspiration for me in the creation of my seasonal presentations.

It was also Jane who expanded our collections still further, by commissioning visual artists to share their own inspirations out of paper, feathers, and any other materials that struck their fancy (Figs. 6–7). I love those designs in particular; what better way to express my lifelong conviction that beautiful shoes are truly an art form unto themselves?

7
Linda Leviton (active 1993–present)
Ribbon Candy,
undated
Wire
Photo by Lucas Zarebinski
Collection of Jane Gershon Weitzman

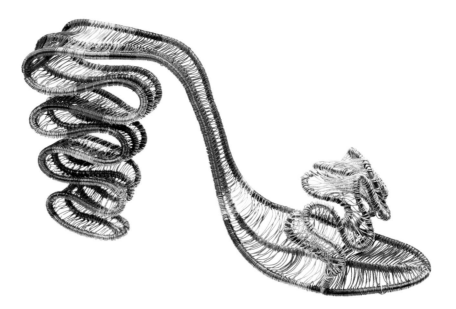

STANDING IN HEELS, STANDING ON PRINCIPLE?

VALERIE PALEY
Director, Center for Women's History
Vice President and Chief Historian,
New-York Historical Society

[previous page]
Seymour Weitzman,
designer
Mr. Seymour
Pointed-toe pumps,
ca. 1964
Leather, rhinestones
Stuart Weitzman
Collection, no. 270
(Fig. 143)

In 1980, the iconic entertainer Bette Midler reflected on her passion for shoes, avowing a preference for the spike-heeled variety. Back then, stilettos were not to be found everywhere, and in every price range, as would become the case a decade or two later. "I firmly believe that with the right footwear, one can rule the world," Midler asserted. "Fortunately for the world," she added, "I have not found the correct footwear to achieve that goal."[1]

As a woman in the sober profession of history and a proud (albeit height-challenged) wearer of high heels myself, I find this cheerful admission from as bold a feminist as Midler somewhat reassuring. So often, one reads of how women's shoes can imprison instead of empower: heels, in particular, being an oppressive and uncomfortable fashion choice serving no constructive purpose other than to appeal to the baser instincts of heterosexual men. But some women would have it the other way around—that in high heels, one, indeed, can rule the world.

Everyone on the planet—with few exceptions—wears something to protect the soft skin of the foot from the hard crust of the earth. But shoes in recent years also have culturally transcended their utilitarian purpose to become an object of desire and deliberation, calling up larger, more abstract ideological considerations—like the freighted meanings of femininity, power, domination, and ambition—for both women and men alike. How did the original function of the heel—to elevate the male aristocrat—rise symbolically to such gendered heights?

To be clear, the high heel is not strictly a type of shoe—it is a form of heel affixed to a shoe that in its most straightforward function increases physical height, while also impacting the body in other ways. High heels both elongate and draw attention to the leg. They alter pelvic movement and gait. They force the back to sway, pitching the chest forward and the buttocks backward. The implication is that women wear high heels to enhance sexual attraction and viscerally broadcast their allure and vulnerability. Teetering some five inches off the ground and taking short strides with unavoidably oscillating hips, a woman cannot walk too fast or too far in heels—catnip to a man with knight-on-a-white-horse aspirations, or less noble designs.

Shoes, nevertheless, also serve both transformative and performative purposes. Apart from completing an outfit's "look," footwear can help convey subtle—and not-so-subtle—messages about one's character, or, at least, the role a wearer has decided to play at a certain moment. Whether "dressed for success," "dressed to kill," or "dressed down," a woman completes the impression with what she opts to put on her feet. In her daily comings and goings, does she strut, march, stand firm, or race about? Does she want the sound of her shoes to herald her arrival prior to making an appearance, like Bette Davis, who disdained "pussyfooting"? The thought-provoking possibilities—and their implications—are endless.

Nevertheless, footwear and feminism are uneasy bedfellows. In terms of clothing, perhaps only the brassiere competes with shoes for ink spilled in the discussion of patriarchal oppression. Did men have a systematic plan in mind when they designed the thoroughly impractical high-heeled shoe and then forced women to wear them, based on what they and their male brethren thought looked most titillating? Or do women break free of patriarchal control when they wear high heels, by embracing a heady mix of power, sexuality, and domination? Or, maybe, do they succumb to it?

While some fashion historians would credit the heel's centrality in the politics of dress in relation to the early-twentieth-century debate over women's right to vote—connecting suffering feet, ironically, with suffrage and the peculiar zeitgeists of politics and fashion, others would support the assumption that women's selections always have had an eye on the "male gaze."[2] For still other observers, it's a matter of choice: women today are presented with a wide range of styles of footwear and the free will to wear whatever they jolly well please, for their own personal reasons. Or, in the words of writer and former model Jenna Sauers in the blog *Jezebel*, "Feminism has less to do with what you put on your feet than what you put in your head."[3]

The shoe designer Stuart Weitzman comprehends this debate in his work, which, among other things, boasts several different styles of toe boxes—sometimes adapted to the same shoe—to suit women's comfort and tastes first, not men's. He grew up in the shoe business and embarked on a career as a designer in the 1960s, a time during which the *New York Times* would declare the industry "archaic" and without funds for design, research, or development.[4] To add insult to injury, a flood of cheap imports further impaired American shoemaking in the 1970s and 80s, causing more than half of the nation's 1,100 plants to close.[5] In the ensuing decades, Weitzman would belie these dreary reports by himself cultivating a keen awareness and promotion

of the history and background of footwear design and manufacturing—which in 2016 constituted an American market of almost $80 billion.[6] Indeed, the narrative of shoes—past, present, and future—is fundamental to who he is.

Part of that story is the acknowledged leadership of men in an industry catering to women. There are some exceptions. Beth Levine, for example, was both the brains and the brawn behind a shoe empire named for her husband and business partner, Herbert Levine. As America's "First Lady of Shoe Design," she shod, among others, American first ladies, film actresses (Barbra Streisand in *Funny Girl*), and 1960s go-go dancers, whose boots were made for both walking *and* dancing.[7] The winner of numerous design awards, she confessed that the company, however, was called Herbert Levine because "the name sounded like a shoemaker." But its innovations, like the slingback, which helped the high-heeled slipper transition from the private boudoir to the public arena, were all hers.[8] Beth Levine's personal history echoes the story of many striving young women of the early twentieth century: the daughter of immigrants, she found work and independence in Manhattan in the 1930s. Beginning as a shoe model, she rose to stylist, then designer, then head designer for I. Miller, the storied American shoe company, which itself would be led by a woman, Geraldine Stutz, in the 1950s.

In fact, scratch the surface, and there is more to the larger story of women and shoes than meets the eye. Aiding what Beth Levine called "the gentle craft" of shoemaking was a substantial workforce of women, engaged at sewing machines in factories throughout the United States (Fig. 8). During the early twentieth century, when the national average of working women across all industries was just shy of 20 percent, over one-third of the shoe industry's workforce was female.[9] Their finished products would be shipped to department stores, themselves temples of social aspiration and feminine independence, where, beginning in the mid- to late nineteenth century, women could work as sales clerks, mingle and shop unchaperoned, and become part of a larger consumer culture (Fig. 9). And sometimes, the force behind the retail enterprise might be an unknown female entrepreneur, like Mary Ann Cohen Magnin, who in 1877 named her fashionable women's department store I. Magnin, after her husband, Isaac. His own particular passions happened to be socialism and philosophy—and not business—which he left up to his wife.[10]

Indeed, as producers, consumers, and leaders, women have not been entirely passive players in the saga of shoes. It is thus fitting that the Stuart Weitzman Collection of Historic Footwear was in fact assembled by a woman, Jane Gershon Weitzman, his wife. To hear the designer explain the collection's origins, it would seem that his wife's choices were about as politically charged as the act of buying her husband a new necktie for a special occasion. The antique and vintage shoes just simply were obtainable—at auction and elsewhere—and enticingly beautiful. Over time the collection would take on an encyclopedic quality, but propelled, for the most part, by aesthetic appeal.

The heels, in particular, are spectacular. Their structure and detailing, as Edward Maeder explains in this volume, were the results of myriad forces in politics, design, and technology. As the bespoke creations of a humbler era made way for the explosion of mass production in the twentieth century, shoes took on a new social significance—easily available and affordable accessories that could be counted upon as the finishing touch of an integrated and personally defining fashion ensemble.

Plainly, we are talking about *women's* footwear here. By and large, men's shoes, regardless of design, have a standard-issue, flat, "practical" quality predicated on comfort. It is no doubt for this reason—their "male" characteristics—that such shoes typically have been associated with power. High heels, on the other hand, in all their impractical, sexy, and uncomfortable glory, are typically associated with femininity and fantasy. Think: the glass or ruby slippers of Cinderella and Dorothy; or Hans Christian Andersen's demonic "red shoes" (or the even more ghoulish unnatural feet that the Little Mermaid magically sprouts, causing her unspeakable, knife-like pain).

From time to time, men have tried on higher heels to see if the shoe fits, so to speak. Rock stars from David Bowie to Prince most famously have sported them. But so, too, have others. Interestingly, and drag queens notwithstanding, as recently as 2011 in New York, gentlemen technically could be arrested (invoking a nineteenth-century law) for wearing clothing that suggested the impersonation of a female.[11] Yet in the early 1970s, young African American men from Harlem were credited with starting a wider shoe craze for heels among their urban confreres (Fig. 10). The trend had little to do with trying to look taller. Nor was it a particularly gay fad, according to the *New York Times*: "Rather the shoes can give the wearer that tough swagger of the cowboy," the article explained—the lift of cowboy boots, of course, being a tad more predictably mainstream.[12]

And maybe it is something of that swagger that women appreciate in their stilettos. Technology of the 1950s and the ingenuity of Italian shoemakers enabled this design, which makes use of a metal stick rammed into the shoe heel to prevent breakage. This facilitated thinner, stronger, higher heels. Even forgetting the fact that *stiletto* is Italian for "dagger," the sharp symbolism of weaponry, power, height, and, yes, pain, is, well, staggering. And if the imagery of a dominatrix doesn't necessarily spring to mind, still, in the early twenty-first century, it is safe to say that the purchase, collecting, and appreciation of women's shoes approach fetish-worthy levels.

Which brings us back to Stuart Weitzman. In the 2010s, a perfect storm of spandex technology, changing styles, social coding, and female preference prompted him to think about adapting the over-the-knee boot—long the fashion choice of women in the X-rated professions—for a more conventional consumer, by varying the customary heel and toe designs. The resulting popularity of the footwear formerly known as "hooker boots" and their growing ubiquity in polite company is testament to Weitzman's sensibilities. Whether the idea of these boots will soon be considered as empowering to women as the combat boot remains up for debate. But in the end, to paraphrase one sage, perhaps sometimes maybe a boot is just a boot.

10
New York street scene, 1975
Anthony Barboza /
Getty Images

FASHION, PERFORMANCE, AND POLITICS

An Introduction to the Stuart Weitzman Collection

EDWARD MAEDER
Costume and textile historian

[previous page]
Evening sandals,
ca. 1945
Silk, leather
Stuart Weitzman
Collection, no. 42
(Fig. 92)

Having been a scholar of costume for the duration of my career—most notably as the Curator of Costume and Textiles at the Los Angeles County Museum of Art, and the Founding Director of the Bata Shoe Museum in Toronto—I was delighted to have the opportunity to organize, conserve, research, and write about Stuart Weitzman's charming and extensive collection of footwear. Dress holds the key to our perception of who we think we are—and who we want to be. We believe that our clothes cover us, when in fact they reveal our true selves.[1] As the British costume historian Stella Mary Newton observed, our clothing provides a probing means of communication "as silently we inspect one another,"[2] while contemporary fashion historian Caroline Cox writes, "Shoes, like clothes, have the shape-shifting ability to reflect each decade's zeitgeist."[3] Indeed, as Stuart Weitzman, and anyone who studies the history of fashion, well knows, clothing—and footwear—is the perhaps the most accurate social and cultural indicator of any time period. Fashion can instantly communicate status, age, gender, ethnicity, social, religious, and cultural pressures on individuals and societies, as well as the aspirations, preoccupations, aesthetics, and fantasies of any given age.

This insight is reflected in the Weitzman collection, which spans nearly two hundred years and features around three hundred pairs of footwear that represent primarily American and European high fashion from before the American Civil War to the robust and international world of the 1980s. Interspersed with these are some beautiful examples of shoes, boots, and slippers from China, India, Turkey, and the Middle East. Stuart Weitzman began his career as a leading shoe designer in American fashion in the 1960s. Over a number of years he acquired examples of chic footwear from many sources, including other designers and principally through gifts from his wife, Jane Gershon Weitzman. The selections in this volume reveal the Weitzmans' refined aesthetics, their eye for originality, and their insider's sense of what makes a successful shoe design, including opulent materials and decoration, striking silhouettes, and comfortable construction. At the same time, the shoes illustrated here mirror the themes of modern popular life: they reveal our fads in dance, passion for movies, and tastes from the Jazz Age and Art Deco to Pop and postmodernism; they evoke political and social concerns from Prohibition to women's suffrage and equal rights, from femininity to feminism.

11 [opposite]
Actress Laura
Harring at the 74th
Annual Academy
Awards, 2002
© Academy of Motion
Picture Arts and
Sciences & ABC, Inc. /
Photofest

Stuart Weitzman has not only preserved an important facet of costume history, but he has also continued to move fashion's trajectory by constant innovations in his own footwear, which is worn by many of the most fashionable women of our time. Indeed, at the 2002 Academy Awards, Weitzman's "Million dollar sandals" (Fig. 11), set with 464 Kwiat diamonds, generated so much excitement when worn by Laura Elena Harring, then co-starring in David Lynch's critically acclaimed *Mulholland Dr.*, that organizers were persuaded to install a floor-level camera on the red carpet, bringing new interest to fashion footwear worldwide.

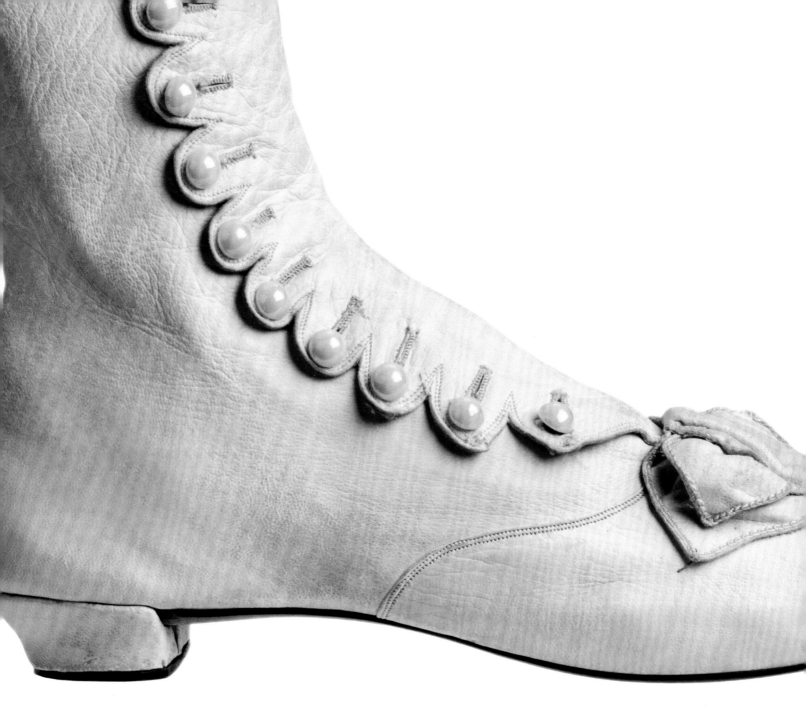

SENTIMENTAL SURVIVORS

The earliest example in the Stuart Weitzman Collection is a pair of bridal shoes (Fig. 12) worn in 1838 by Caroline Howard for her marriage in Boston to Rev. Thomas Marsh Clark (later Bishop of Rhode Island). At this time, shoe soles were shaped as so-called straights, with no distinction between the left and the right foot. There are various explanations for this indifference to the mirrored shapes of feet, and one of them is ancient. The early Christian church decreed that shoes displaying the forms of feet were sensual and therefore forbidden. "The shoe's purpose is hiding," writes fashion historian Bernard Rudofsky. "The Christian idea of shoes was to achieve near-oblivion for the foot. Every respect for anatomical reality was abandoned, and the shoe was built on the most rigid principles of symmetry."[4] This taboo disappeared later on, but reappeared in certain shoes from the sixteenth through the mid-nineteenth century. At the beginning of the nineteenth century, when less structured shoes for ladies were stylish, "straights" also simplified production.

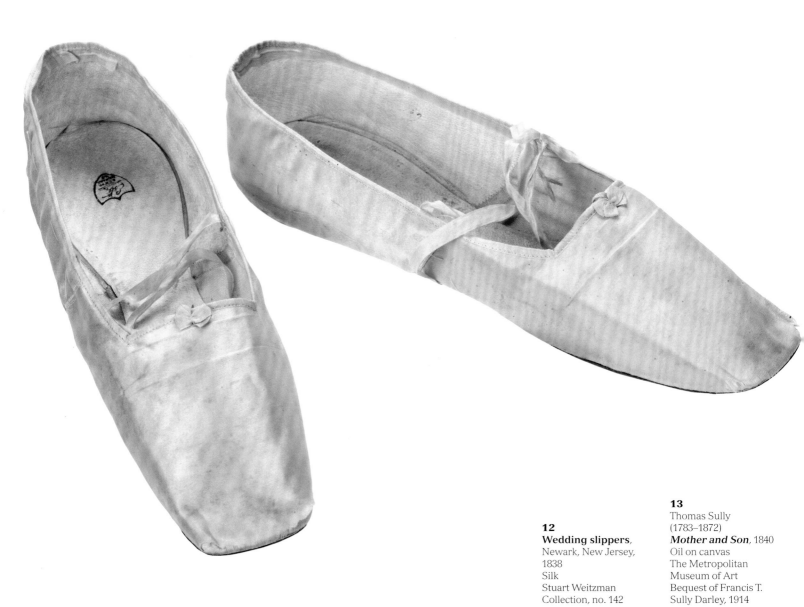

12
Wedding slippers,
Newark, New Jersey,
1838
Silk
Stuart Weitzman
Collection, no. 142

13
Thomas Sully
(1783–1872)
Mother and Son, 1840
Oil on canvas
The Metropolitan
Museum of Art
Bequest of Francis T.
Sully Darley, 1914

Caroline Howard Clark's simple, thin, and fragile slippers are typical of this period (Figs. 13–14). They signaled status, as their owners' homes must have boasted Brussels wool carpets over the wooden floors to keep shoes from wearing out too quickly (Fig. 15). Such impractical styles were heartily ridiculed by the English writer Frances Trollope when she lived and traveled in the new nation from 1828 to 1831. American women, she sniffed, "never wear muffs or boots, and appear extremely shocked at the sight of comfortable walking shoes and cotton stockings, even when they have to step to their sleighs over ice and snow."[5]

The history of elevated footwear is a long and complex story that may have originated in the height-enhancing shoes worn by ancient Greek performers to improve their visibility in the amphitheater. Elevated shoes reappeared in the Renaissance and were called "chopines" by Venetian courtesans. This was followed by an entirely different means of adding stature—the high heel—which can be traced back to the tenth century, when Persian horseback riders used the device to anchor their boots in their stirrups as a practical measure.[6]

The Last & Newest Fashions, 1838. Evening & Morning Dresses. (1)

14
***The Last & Newest
Fashions, 1838.
Evening & Morning
Dresses***
Hand-colored engraving
*The World of Fashion
and Continental
Feuilletons*, vol. 15, pl. 1,
January 1838
London: John Bell
Irene Lewisohn
Costume Reference
Library, The
Metropolitan Museum
of Art

15
Attributed to George W.
Twibill Jr. (1806–1836)
***The Family of John Q.
Aymar***, ca. 1833
Oil on canvas
The Metropolitan
Museum of Art
Gift of A. Grima
Johnson, 2008

High heels became fashionable in the late seventeenth century, as legend has it, when Princess Henrietta Anne of England mocked her husband, Monsieur Philippe, brother of King Louis XIV of France, for his short stature. In reaction, Philippe added two-inch heels to his shoes, leading the Sun King, who is believed to have been about five and a half feet tall, to copy the innovation. This most extravagant of Bourbon monarchs used red leather for the heel and extended it up to five inches, spurring courtiers across Europe to adopt this literal "height" of fashion (Fig. 16).[7]

Beyond increasing the wearer's height, high heels have the additional benefit of making the calf muscles flex, producing a more curvaceous and longer line in the leg, and visually minimizing the apparent size of the foot. The various styles of knee breeches of the Baroque and Rococo periods and the fashion for court dancing assisted in this display. The disadvantage of towering heels, however, was insecure walking—despite that fact that the precarious undulations induced by high heels appealed to many onlookers. As an eighteenth-century satirist quipped: "Mount on French heels when you go to a ball, it now is the fashion to totter and fall."[8]

An early example of modest heels in the Weitzman Collection is seen in a pair of "boudoir shoes," a style worn by ladies in the privacy of their own homes and said to have entered England and the Continent from Turkey in the early eighteenth century.[9] A rare pair, these shoes are embroidered in

16 [opposite]
Hyacinthe Rigaud
(1659–1743)
*Portrait of Louis XIV
(1638-1715), King of
France*, 1701
Oil on canvas
Musée du Louvre

17 [left]
François Hubert
Ponscarme (1827–1903)
**Prize medal,
Exposition
Universelle, Paris,**
1867
Copper alloy
Private collection

18 [below]
Shoes, 1867
Silk, embroidery,
metallic thread
Stuart Weitzman
Collection, no. 101

The detail shows the
exhibition seal stamped
on the soles.

the Turkish style and clearly stamped with a seal of excellence from the Paris Exposition Universelle of 1867, indicating the Orientalist allure of *turquerie*, with its aura of the harem (Figs. 17–18, 20). A slingback form, with a strap around the heel, can be seen in a Weitzman Collection example (Fig. 19).

The earliest outdoor footwear with heels in the collection is a lady's typical high-button boot of white kid leather from about 1870 (Fig. 21). This style had been widely used for more than a generation and would continue to be popular in various forms well into the twentieth century (Figs. 22–23). Such boots of the Victorian era would have peeped out from long dresses with bell-shaped skirts supported by crinolines over stiff hoops, and from mid-century onward, princess-line dresses outfitted with

LES MODES PARISIENNES PETERSON'S MAGAZINE.
NOVEMBER 1867.

19 [opposite]
Slingback slippers,
1890s
Silk, elastic, beads
Stuart Weitzman
Collection, no. 167

20 [left]
Les Modes
Parisiennes
Hand-colored
engraving
Peterson's Magazine,
November 1867
New-York Historical
Society Library

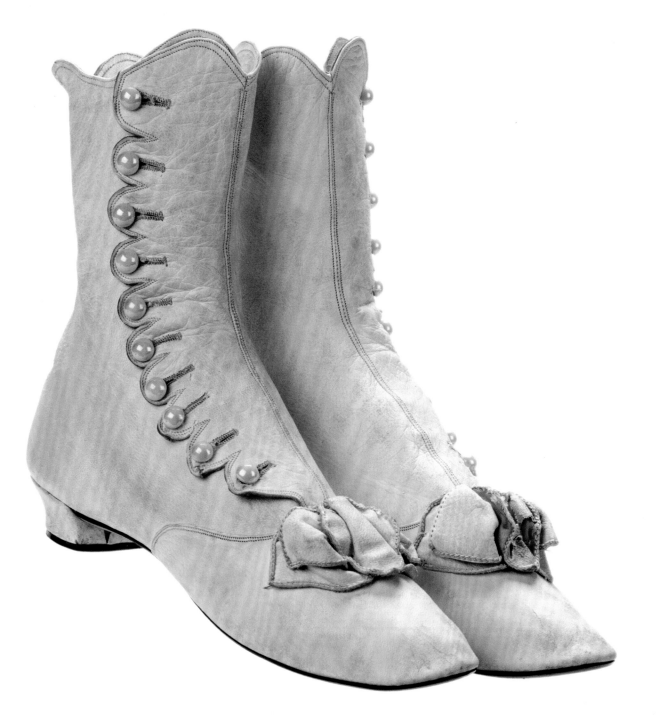

cumbersome trains. In fact, the lady's boot may have evolved for modesty. As she negotiated doorways, crowds, and coach steps, she had to lift her hoop skirts to avoid their swaying upward, putting her in danger of revealing her ankles.[10] Ironically, a tightly laced boot came to be seen as erotically charged. Victorian women were also seemingly plagued with the chronic problem of "weak ankles," and boots were a practical and stylish solution.[11] Whatever their source, lightweight, low-heeled boots proved to be perfect for both indoors and out, for short promenades. However, in inclement weather a lady would choose more practical boots of stronger leather.

Because boots of kid leather and other more formal shoes were far from robust, their very survival is in itself surprising. Unless they were preserved as mementos of important occasions—like Mrs. Clark's silk wedding slippers of 1838—such delicate items may have survived because they were extremely small and, despite being handed down to succeeding generations, unwearable. Shoes were also saved because fashions changed before they could be worn out, or they were kept by their makers as samples or exhibition entries, or they were oddities that attracted the whimsy of collectors.[12]

21 [opposite]
Buttoned boots, 1870s
Leather
Stuart Weitzman
Collection, no. 179

22 [above]
Hans & Nix / The Drummer Girls,
ca. 1908
Lithograph
Cincinnati: Enquirer Job
Printing Co.
Courtesy of Swann
Auction Galleries

23
Lace-up boots, ca. 1900
Silk and silk brocade
Stuart Weitzman
Collection, no. 59

24
Ladies' Fine Shoes
Sears, Roebuck & Co.,
1897
Reprinted, New York:
Chelsea House, 1968
New-York Historical
Society Library

The Industrial Revolution gradually mechanized the production of shoes like so many other consumer goods. At the same time, department stores emerged as big city emporiums of fashion to attract an acquisitive, growing middle class. Regarding apparel in general, and footwear in particular, high-quality design in mechanized production began to blur the social distinctions conferred by custom couture in the era of handicrafts. As the American population expanded, pleasingly styled and economically priced shoes and boots for both sexes became increasingly available— the kind that could be bought through mail-order catalogues, like those produced by Montgomery Ward and Sears, Roebuck (Fig. 24). By the late nineteenth century, the stage was set for fashions in footwear to become a popular form of expression pursued across class levels, especially in America, where New England's mass manufacturing dominated even transatlantic shoe production (Figs. 25– 26).[13] Like all forms of dress, shoes would be shaped by mass culture, advancing technology, and the demand for practicality, in addition to high styles. Primarily mass-produced in the twentieth century, the Weitzman collection shoes that follow are both fashionable and functional. Their shape, design, manufacture, and materials all reflect the fads, follies, and functional requirements of their respective epoch.

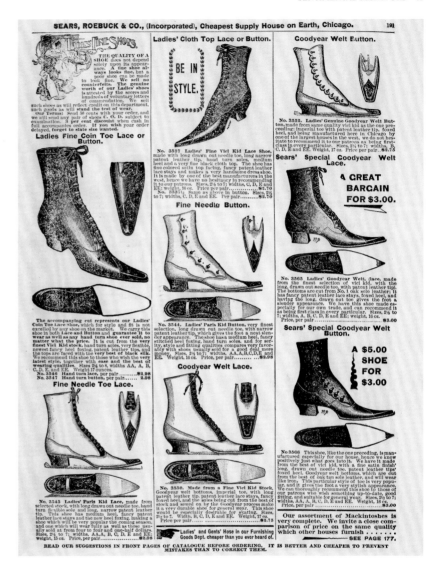

25
Shoes, ca. 1870s
Kid leather
Stuart Weitzman
Collection, no. 129

26
Buttoned shoes,
1870–80
Leather, buttons
Stuart Weitzman
Collection, no. 60

POLITICS AND PROSPERITY FROM THE GROUND UP

Hierarchical and religious regimes have made their power felt through sumptuary laws and edicts on dress. In medieval Italy, for example, regulations forbade the wearing of certain exaggerated styles, such as ultra-tall headdresses and shoes with extremely long toes. In the guise of reining in extravagance, such codes reminded people of their social place. In seventeenth-century colonial New England, Puritan leaders frowned on garments with lace, jewels, and other costly imports. However, authority was later met with rebellion. Perhaps the most dramatic social defiance in modern American history occurred after the Great War with two Constitutional amendments.

In 1919, following nearly a century of ferment, Prohibition was ratified by the Eighteenth Amendment to the U.S. Constitution. Forbidding alcohol consumption quickly created a vast underground network of speakeasies and clandestine dance halls and clubs, where revelers drank, danced, and flouted the law. Together with the Nineteenth Amendment granting women the right to vote, these laws helped create the New Woman of the Roaring Twenties. News photographs of suffragists had already shown that women were wearing practical as well as modish shoes and boots as they marched through city streets to demand votes for women (Figs. 27–34). Their new freedom, as ratified by their vote, became the basis for a groundswell of rapidly changing fashions that would thrust women's footwear into the limelight for the first time.

Adding to these influences was the astonishing prosperity of the 1920s, fueled by consumer spending and speculation in real estate and the stock market.[14] Automobile magnate Henry Ford had already startled the nation by doubling his workers' wages to an unprecedented $5 a day. In 1919 he raised the wage again, to $6. After saving for four months each worker could buy one of the cars he had made.[15]

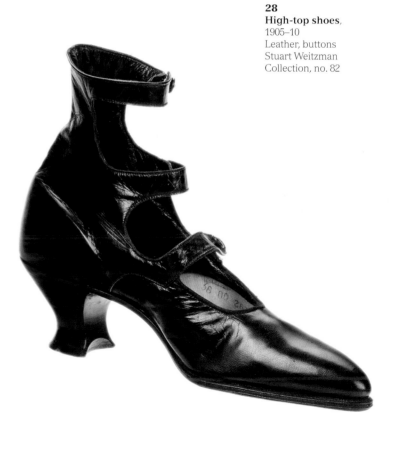

27
Hilda M. Dallas
(1878–1958)
*Votes for Women 1d. /
Wanted Everywhere*,
1909
Lithograph
Schlesinger Library on
the History of Women in
America
Radcliffe Institute
for Advanced Study,
Harvard University

28
High-top shoes,
1905–10
Leather, buttons
Stuart Weitzman
Collection, no. 82

29
Buttoned boots,
ca. 1920
Leather, felt, buttons
Stuart Weitzman
Collection, no. 85

30
Buttoned boots,
ca. 1918
Leather, buttons
Stuart Weitzman
Collection, no. 28

Twenties' fashions expressed a similar ebullience. "Women's skirts, for centuries at ankle or lower length, rose scandalously to knee height, shockingly exposing legs," writes shoe historian William Rossi. Thus was born the association between short hems and stock market highs. "Society's traditional rules of behavior," already undermined by the wide rebellion against Prohibition, "appeared to be on a roller coaster to hell," Rossi explains. "As women's legs emerged from the dark, they became a major focal site of attraction. . . . They needed a pedestal of sexy heels to show them off at their shapely best."[16] "Novelty shoes," which emerged in the late nineteenth century among competing manufacturers,[17] generated a subset in the new century known as "Jazzy shoes," and they took off to meet mass demand.[18] Shoes came with multiple crisscrossing straps fastened with buttons, buckles, or bows; peek-a-boo open toes and other cutouts; and combinations of leathers, artificial and genuine snake skins, extravagant trim, and brilliant colors—all available at a wide choice of prices (Figs. 35–52). In the early 1920s, according to industry surveys, most American women bought only three new pairs of shoes a year. One insider complained in 1923 that shoe manufacturers "have not taught our customers to buy shoes for the occasion."[19] That would soon change, however. When chains of shoe stores opened at state and national levels in the Roaring Twenties, shoes could be bought from as little as $6 to $25 a pair (the average weekly wage for a

31
Underwood &
Underwood
Suffrage rally,
April 19, 1917
Photographic print
New-York Historical
Society Library

32
**Red Cross Noiseless
shoes**, ca. 1918
Leather
Stuart Weitzman
Collection, no. 8

33
Lace-up boot,
Portland, Oregon,
1910–15
Leather, canvas, laces
Stuart Weitzman
Collection, no. 20

34
**American Lady Shoe
advertisement**
Published in *The Ladies'
Home Journal*, March
1908
Private collection

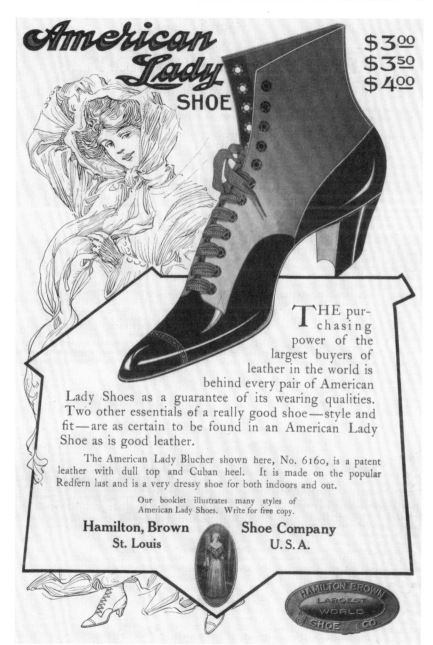

35
Crossed-strap shoes,
ca. 1912–14
Leather, gold beads
Stuart Weitzman
Collection, no. 6

36
**Jean Rai, a Lido Club
dancer, performs the
Black Bottom Blues**,
undated
© Hulton-Deutsch
Collection / Corbis /
Getty Images

37
John Held Jr.
(1889–1958)
*Teaching Old Dogs
New Tricks*
Cover, *Life* magazine,
February 18, 1928
New-York Historical
Society Library

female clerk or secretary was about $13 in the mid-1920s).[20]

Geometrically constructed dresses that disregarded the female form were fashion's latest surprise, and they moved with the wearer's performance of the frenetic new dances. Beads and embroidery in silver and gold as well as flapping fringes swirled across America's dance floors to the new and exciting sounds of modern music. Shoes made of gleaming satins in silk and rayon, metallic brocades, and gilded kid, with sequins and beads of glass and cut steel, caught the dance hall's light as flappers trotted out steps never seen before (Figs. 36–37, see also pages 77–103).

38
Shoes, ca. 1912
Leather, beads, sequins
Stuart Weitzman
Collection, no. 220

39
Crossed-strap shoes,
ca. 1914
Silk, beads, pearls,
buttons
Stuart Weitzman
Collection, no. 221

40
Shoes, ca. 1914
Silk, elastic, beads
Stuart Weitzman
Collection, no. 63

41
Pumps, ca. 1915
Kid leather, steel-cut
beads, marquisettes,
buttons
Stuart Weitzman
Collection, no. 219

42
Pumps, ca. 1915
Kid leather, glass beads,
blue glass paillettes,
buttons
Stuart Weitzman
Collection, no. 222

43
Spectator pumps,
ca. 1915
Leather
Stuart Weitzman
Collection, no. 26

44
**Pointed-toe Mary
Jane shoes**, ca. 1916
Suede, leather, buttons
Stuart Weitzman
Collection, no. 75

45
Mary Jane shoes,
1920s
Snakeskin, kid leather,
cording
Stuart Weitzman
Collection, no. 86

46
Pumps, ca. 1920
Cloth of gold
Stuart Weitzman
Collection, no. 61

47
Four-button shoes,
early 1920s
Leather, beads, buttons
Stuart Weitzman
Collection, no. 27

48
Crossed-strap shoes,
1920s
Kid leather, buttons
Stuart Weitzman
Collection, no. 143

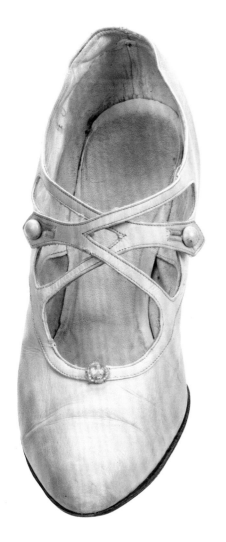

49
Pumps, late 1920s
Silk brocade, kid leather
Stuart Weitzman
Collection, no. 247

50
**D'Orsay evening
shoes**, ca. 1928
Silk brocade, kid leather,
rhinestones, beads,
buttons
Stuart Weitzman
Collection, no. 153

51
Mary Jane shoes,
ca. 1926
Brocade, buttons
Stuart Weitzman
Collection, no. 164

52
Spectator shoes,
ca. 1928
Kid leather and suede,
mother-of-pearl buttons
Stuart Weitzman
Collection, no. 196

POPULAR DANCES FOCUS ON FEET

Popular culture of the 1920s boasted a succession of new dances, yet perhaps none summarized the decade better than the Charleston (Fig. 53). With its rapid beat and gyrating steps, this athletic dance captured America's attention from its introduction in 1923. Contests were held from coast to coast, and winners were featured in an emerging genre of mass-circulation magazines dedicated to entertainment. A 1926 competition in Manhattan showcased nine women displaying their prizewinning legs—and, of course, the shoes that flattered them (Fig. 54). The various shoe styles, shapes, materials, and decorations in this tabloid news photograph are reflected in several exceptional examples in the Weitzman Collection (Figs. 55–57, 61).

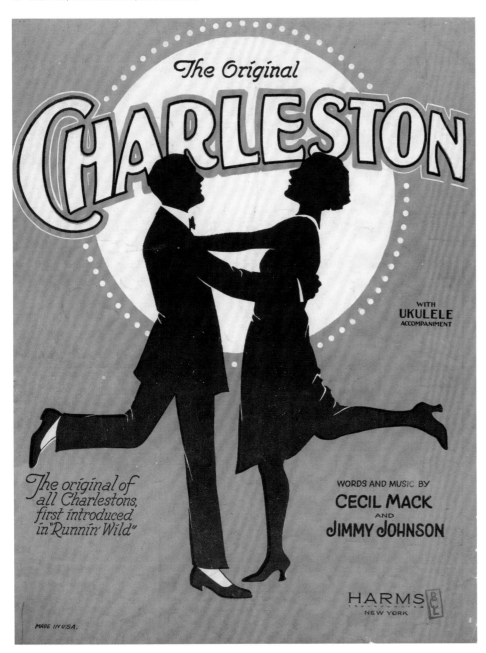

53
The Original Charleston
Sheet music
New York: Harms Inc., 1923
New-York Historical Society Library

54
Charleston champions invade New York, 1926
New York Daily News Archive / Getty Images

Such an exciting new dance, when combined with women's "liberated" limbs and the effects of illicit alcohol (concealed in men's "bootleg" flasks), made an extreme impact on the generally conservative U.S. public. Buying cars "on time"—that is, in installments—introduced the concept of "buy now, pay later" to those with limited buying power. The same idea seemed to spread across society, translated into "play now, pay later" to lower-income consumers. And play they did. Women bobbed their hair, smoked cigarettes, rouged their knees (which were visible for the first time in history), drank to excess, toyed with "free love," and—if they could afford it—spent a high percentage of their income on a stream of chic new shoes.

The twentieth century had already seen the debut of dances that allowed couples to publicly embrace one another and move cheek to cheek, in a shock to social mores of the time. In 1912, former president Theodore Roosevelt's

55
Diagonal-strap shoes,
Chicago, ca. 1927
Suede, leather,
embroidery, Dr. Scholl's
"Walk Strate" patented
heel pads
Stuart Weitzman
Collection, no. 38

56
Mary Jane shoes,
ca. 1930
Metallic brocade, kid
leather, mother-of-pearl
buttons
Stuart Weitzman
Collection, no. 55

daughter, Alice Longworth, introduced the ragtime turkey trot to Washington, DC, at a dance given by Mrs. Robert Patterson for her daughter, the Countess Eleanor Gizycki.[21] Such society endorsements lessened the scandal of these dances. Youth culture with its liberated mores was taking over popular dance and music: the decorous waltz ceded to dances with animal names, like the bunny hug and the fox-trot.[22]

Changes in women's fashions exposed dancing feet in new ways (Fig. 58). Introduced in 1913, the fox-trot is believed to have been named for comedian Harry Fox of the *Ziegfeld Follies*, and it was popularized by Vernon and Irene Castle in Irving Berlin's suitably named musical *Watch Your Step* of 1914 (Fig. 59).[23] The fox-trot was quickly outmoded by the tango, a South American dance that had evolved there several decades earlier and had enchanted tourists to Cuba. "Cuban heels" appeared in this prewar period, with straight lines offering an alternative to curvy, French-sourced "Louis" heels (Fig. 65).

Meanwhile, dancing couples, previously seen only on the vaudeville stage, migrated uptown, to the supper clubs where patrons could dance in addition to dining on fine food accompanied by wine and spirits. Sheet-music illustrations glorified these duos, the lady sometimes appearing in a hobble skirt, sometimes in less restrictive styles that showed off the new dance steps (Figs. 62–64, 67).

57
Pumps, ca. 1930
Leather
Stuart Weitzman
Collection, no. 173

58
Clara Bow, 1926
Isabel Santos Pilot
(ondiraiduveau) / Flickr

Dance vogues continued through the economic disasters of the 1929 stock market crash and the Great Depression. Radio broadcast the popular music accompanying such fads, like the Big Apple dance, introduced in 1936. At the same time, newsreels covered dance marathons, in which couples competed to see who would be the last standing in events that could continue over several days, and often much longer. Sometimes the contests moved from dance halls to city streets, like the fourteen miles between downtown Los Angeles and Santa Monica (Fig. 60).[24] Strong, comfortable shoes were essential for such athletics, and they must have been available for the competing dancers to afford them. At the high end, however, the styles of many of the most fashionable shoes from the 1920s through the 1930s channeled the aesthetics of vanguard art movements and modish design trends.

The innovative spirit of dance and art enlivened a range of diverse styles (Figs. 66, 68–79).

59
Frances Benjamin
Johnston (1864–1952)
**Irene Castle (1893–
1969) and Vernon
Castle (1887–1918)**,
ca. 1910
Gelatin silver print
Library of Congress

60
Raeburn Van Buren
*"She shook her
partner and gave him
a shove as the music
started again"*
Published in *The
Saturday Evening Post,*
January 24, 1931
Private collection

61
Pumps, late 1920s
Silk, leather
Stuart Weitzman
Collection, no. 43

62
Reuben Fox-Trot
Sheet music
New York, Chicago, and
London: Jos. W. Stern &
Co., 1914
Newberry Library

63
12th Street Rag
Sheet music
Kansas City, MO: J. W.
Jenkins & Sons, 1919
Courtesy of the Lester
S. Levy Collection of
Sheet Music, Sheridan
Libraries, Johns
Hopkins University

64
Flamin' Mamie
Sheet music
New York: Leo Feist,
1925
York University
Libraries, Clara Thomas
Archives & Special
Collections, John Arpin
Collection, JAC001528

65
Buttoned shoe,
ca. 1915
Leather, beads, buttons
Stuart Weitzman
Collection, no. 25

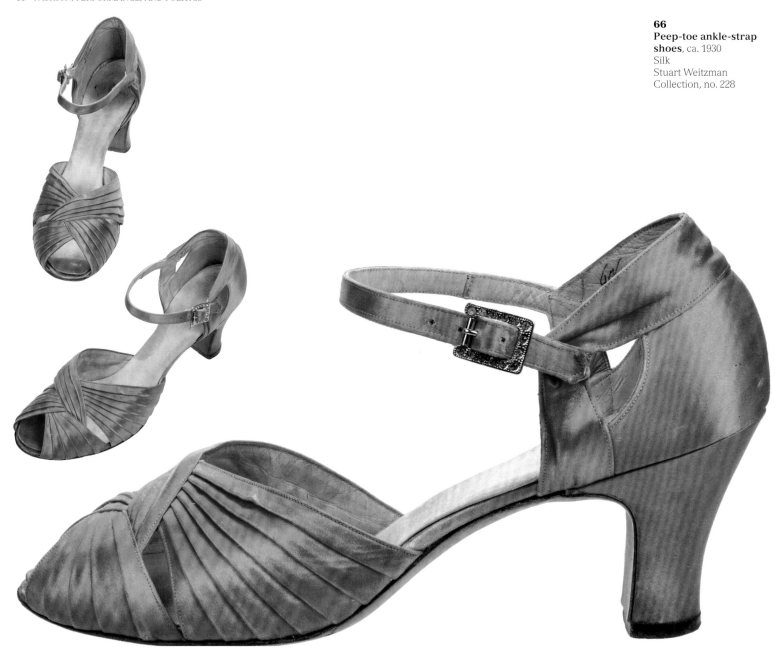

66
**Peep-toe ankle-strap
shoes**, ca. 1930
Silk
Stuart Weitzman
Collection, no. 228

67
Footloose
Sheet music
New York: Sam Fox,
1925
York University
Libraries, Clara Thomas
Archives & Special
Collections, John Arpin
Collection, JAC001522

68
Lace-up shoes,
ca. 1938
Leather, laces
Stuart Weitzman
Collection, no. 203

69
**Peep-toe slingback
evening shoes**, ca. 1938
Velvet, kid leather
Stuart Weitzman
Collection, no. 49

70
**Ankle-strap evening
shoes**, ca. 1935
Velvet, kid leather
Stuart Weitzman
Collection, no. 62

71
**T-strap evening
shoes**, ca. 1938
Faille, kid leather
Stuart Weitzman
Collection, no. 73

72
**D'Orsay evening
shoes**, ca. 1935
Faille, kid leather
Stuart Weitzman
Collection, no. 80

73
Lace-up shoes,
ca. 1935
Linen, laces
Stuart Weitzman
Collection, no. 138

74
D'Orsay shoes,
ca. 1930
Metallic brocade,
kid leather
Stuart Weitzman
Collection, no. 241

75
**Peep-toe platform
sandals**, ca. 1938
Snakeskin, leather
Stuart Weitzman
Collection, no. 89

76
Ankle-strap sandals,
ca. 1930s
Silk, kid leather,
embroidery
Stuart Weitzman
Collection, no. 69

77
T-strap sandals,
ca. 1935
Woven leather, buttons
Stuart Weitzman
Collection, no. 174

78
T-strap pumps,
ca. 1937
Velvet, leather
Stuart Weitzman
Collection, no. 249

79
T-strap shoes, ca. 1936
Leather
Stuart Weitzman
Collection, no. 280

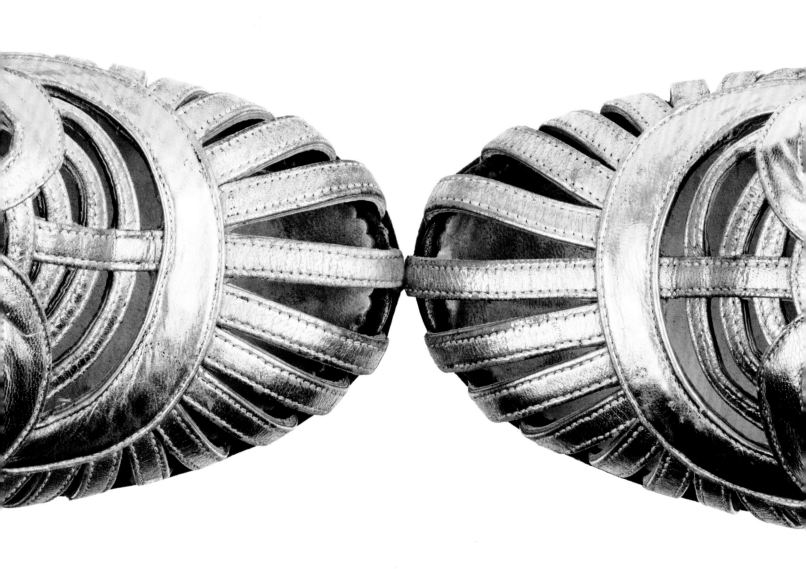

SKYSCRAPER *MODERNE* AND STREAMLINED DESIGNS

Shiny black and gleaming gold is the palette of the American
Radiator Building, erected in 1923–24 and still lording it over
Manhattan's Bryant Park from West 40th Street (Fig. 80); its gold-
toned ceramic decoration and black-glazed brick sheathing remain
both practical and eye-catching. This color pairing had already been
seen in adventurous French couture of the twenties, which flaunted
flat patterns in metallic brocades and printed textiles. Gilded and
silvered kid and black patent leather were the equivalents in footwear;
their ornamentation in arabesques or jagged geometries, like that in
the architecture and furniture later termed Art Deco, derived from
the abstractions of Synthetic Cubism, Purism, and other movements in
avant-garde art (Fig. 81).

In 1930 New York's Chrysler Building briefly held the record as the world's tallest structure, following that of the American Radiator Building (Fig. 82). The chrome-plated hubcap ornaments on its exterior and a spire of silver triangles bursting from successive curves advertised America's luxury car manufacturer, as well as proclaiming 42nd Street the era's center of New York commerce, transport, and entertainment. Women's footwear from this period bears a striking resemblance to this newly developing aesthetic, with rhinestone-studded heels and stylized buckles reflecting architectural inspiration (Figs. 83–87).

Just as the Empire State Building was crowned in 1931 as the world's newest tallest building (a record it would hold for the next forty-two years), John D. Rockefeller Jr. was christening a massive, multi-building complex in midtown Manhattan, named, unsurprisingly, Rockefeller Center. Its skyscrapers were unified by their insistent verticality and silvery, sparingly applied, often streamlined ornament in low relief. Streamlining, the aerodynamic style identified with speed in vehicles from submarines and steamships to racing cars and aircraft, was soon a widely recognized metaphor for America's renewed optimism, and was applied to stationary objects from office buildings to the small, stylish shoes covering women's feet.

80
Raymond Hood,
architect (1881–1934)
**American Radiator
Company building**,
completed 1924
Rendering published in
Architectural Digest,
1950
New-York Historical
Society Library

81
T-strap shoes, ca. 1930
Silk satin, kid leather,
mother-of-pearl buttons
Stuart Weitzman
Collection, no. 41

Decades before the debut of the television series *30 Rock* (the nickname for NBC's headquarters), Rockefeller Center's most famous structure was arguably Radio City Music Hall, opened in 1932. This entertainment center was immediately identified with the nation's apparently Depression-proof film industry, simply known as Hollywood. The "dream machine" of movies had already caught the world's imagination, and marketing publicized the stars' attire with magazine stories, advertising, and department store replicas. Notably, Paris was no longer the sole source of style. American designers such as Adrian, Walter Plunkett, Orry-Kelly, and even a young Edith Head would design garments and commission footwear for Hollywood headliners. Not so subtly, American architecture and film merged to create a changing awareness of beauty based on cinematic spectacle in the decade of the Great Depression. Some of the footwear designed for film would take contemporary fashion to new heights of fantasy.

Aerodynamic lines and verticality inspired many shoe designs of the 1940s, with a hint of the spectacle of cinema (Figs. 88–102).

82
Studio of Irving
Browning (1895–1961)
Chrysler Building,
ca. 1930
Gelatin silver print
New-York Historical
Society Library

83
**Group of decorative
heels**
Wood, rhinestones
Stuart Weitzman
Collection, no.
104.1ab–.6ab

84
**Peep-toe evening
shoes**, ca. 1935
Leather and mesh net
Stuart Weitzman
Collection, no. 3

85
**T-strap evening
shoes**, ca. 1932
Kid leather
Stuart Weitzman
Collection, no. 65

86
**Peep-toe evening
shoes,** late 1930s
Kid leather
Stuart Weitzman
Collection, no. 97

87
**T-strap evening
shoes**, ca. 1931
Silk satin, kid leather
Stuart Weitzman
Collection, no. 124

88
**Peep-toe slingback
shoes**, ca. 1940
Suede, leather
Stuart Weitzman
Collection, no. 250

89
Peep-toe slingback
sandals, ca. 1940
Kid leather
Stuart Weitzman
Collection, no. 234

90
**Peep-toe slingback
shoes**, ca. 1940
Silk, kid leather,
embroidery
Stuart Weitzman
Collection, no. 48

91
Slingback shoes, 1940
Kid leather, mesh,
rhinestones
Stuart Weitzman
Collection, no. 58

92
Evening sandals,
ca. 1945
Silk, leather
Stuart Weitzman
Collection, no. 42

93
Peep-toe laced shoes,
ca. 1941
Suede, laces
Stuart Weitzman
Collection, no. 231

94
Daniel Green shoe advertisement
Published in *Vogue*,
August 15, 1932
Private collection

95
T-strap pumps,
late 1940s
Satin, faille
Stuart Weitzman
Collection, no. 141

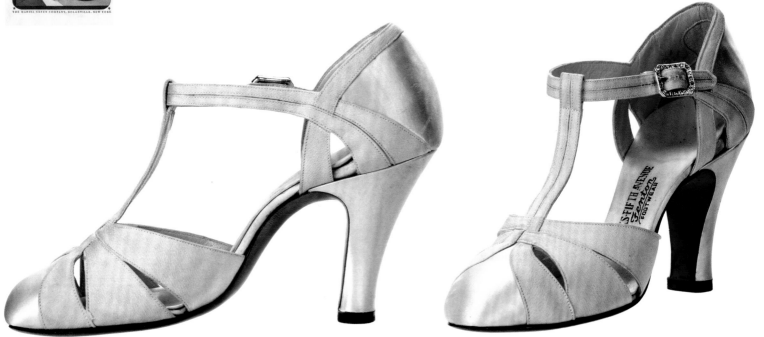

96
**Peep-toe slingback
evening shoes**, 1940s
Leather, elastic
Stuart Weitzman
Collection, no. 88

97
Peep-toe platform shoes, ca. 1945
Suede
Stuart Weitzman
Collection, no. 264

98
**Peep-toe platform
shoes**, ca. 1948
Suede, tack beads
Stuart Weitzman
Collection, no. 256

99
Peep-toe d'Orsay
shoes, ca. 1948
Woven material
Stuart Weitzman
Collection, no. 268

100
Platform shoes,
ca. 1946
Kashmir shawl, beads
Stuart Weitzman
Collection, no. 261

101
Peep-toe slingback evening shoes,
1948–52
Suede
Stuart Weitzman
Collection, no. 123

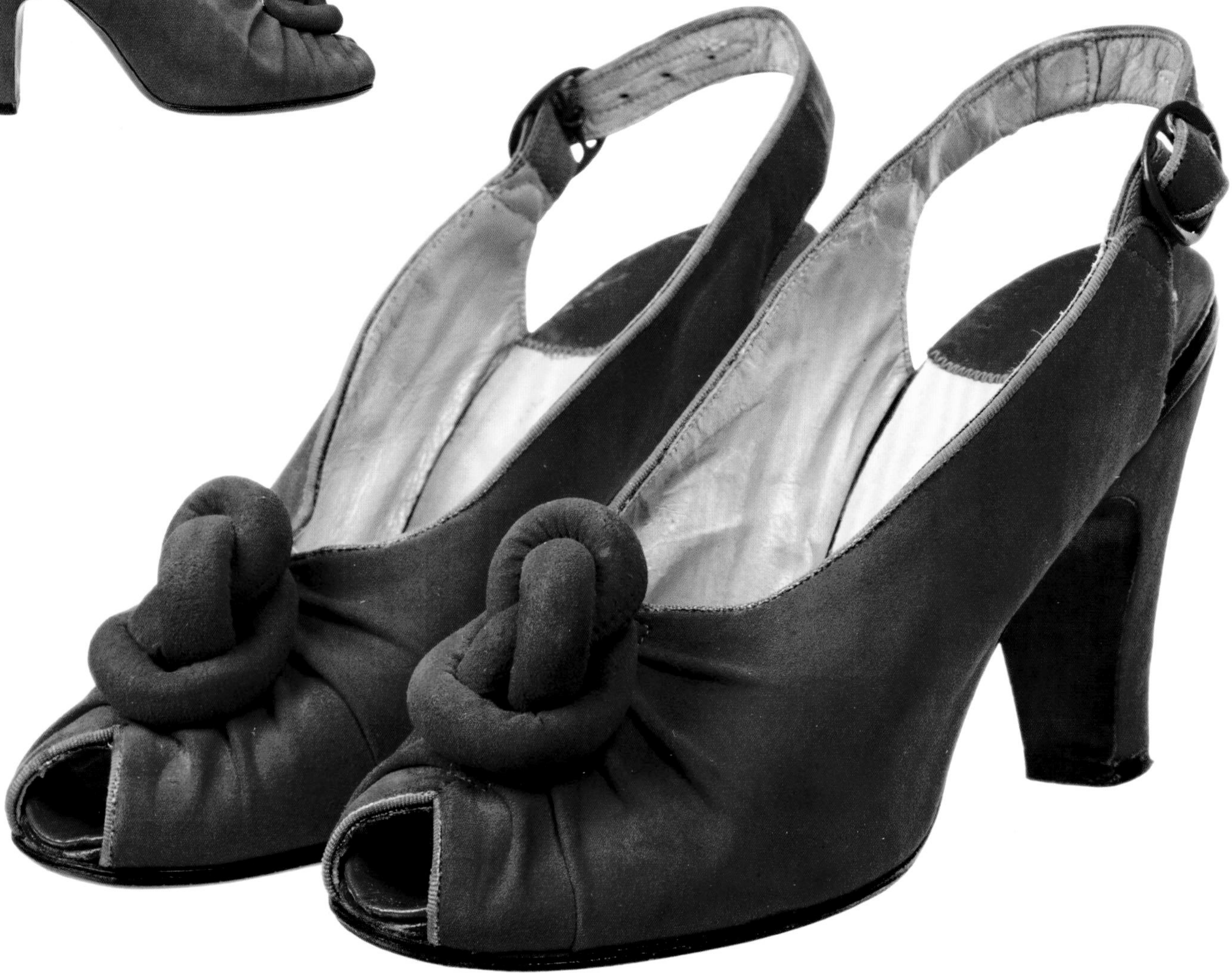

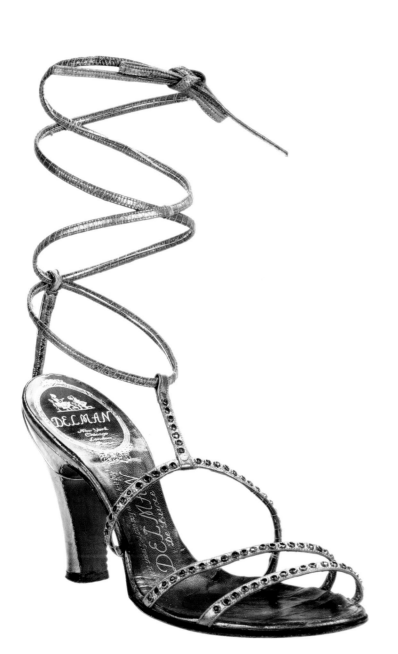

102
Evening sandals,
ca. 1948
Leather, rhinestones
Stuart Weitzman
Collection, no. 5

FILMS AND OTHER IMAGES

Since the introduction of moving pictures in the 1890s, images of larger-than-life heroines have been seared into the collective consciousness, exerting a profound influence on popular taste and aesthetic development. Even in silent films, the levels of glamour radiating from stars like Greta Garbo were often highlighted by their seductive footwear. Stars could be very particular about such accessories. Pola Negri is said to have once stopped production for many hours because her satin shoes did not match the ribbons on her gown. Everything apparently came to a halt until a new pair of shoes could be dyed to match the rest of her outfit exactly. Ironically, the film was in black and white.[25] The famous shoe designer Salvatore Ferragamo began his career in Santa Barbara, California, as a sixteen-year-old from Italy. He was discovered by director D. W. Griffith and

became shoemaker to Mary Pickford, Douglas Fairbanks, and Gloria Swanson, among other great actors of the era (Figs. 103–4). He also shod the principals in Cecil B. DeMille's early Biblical epics. He became a household name through his work in film.[26] Ferragamo's first shoes for Hollywood forecast evening sandals like the luxury brand Palter DeLiso examples in the Weitzman Collection (Fig. 105).

From the late nineteenth century, high fashion has also been shaped by both high society and those who aspire to it, from entertainers to demimondaines. Similarly, fashion followers from the 1930s on could name-drop "Mrs. Simpson" and "Joan Crawford" in almost the same breath. The decade's styles adopted leaner, longer, more body-hugging lines, with impressive shoulder pads, which began to appear near the end of the decade in both daywear and evening gowns. This new silhouette was balanced with platform shoes, which also added height. Paris designer Elsa Schiaparelli paired with Surrealist artist Salvador Dalí to design a hat shaped like a shoe, and is often credited with widening the shoulder while narrowing the waist of women's jackets (Fig. 106).[27] American designer Adrian adapted this silhouette to the broad-shouldered Crawford, who wore high heels with or without platforms, as evidenced by her well-known shoe-closet photos and film scenes (Figs. 107–8). Meanwhile, the American divorcée Wallis Warfield Simpson scandalously married King Edward VIII of Great Britain, which resulted in his abdication in 1936. Her

103
Douglas Fairbanks Sr. in *The Thief of Baghdad*, 1924
© United Artists / Photofest

104
Salvatore Ferragamo, designer
Shoe made for Douglas Fairbanks Sr. in *The Thief of Baghdad*, undated reproduction
Courtesy Museo Salvatore Ferragamo

105
Evening sandals, United States, ca. 1950
Leather, rhinestones
Stuart Weitzman Collection, no. 16

106
Elsa Schiaparelli
(1890–1973)
Shoe hat, 1937–38
Wool
The Metropolitan
Museum of Art
Gift of Rose Messing,
1974

107
Joan Crawford inspects her shoe closet,
ca. 1940s
Hulton Archives / Getty Images

108
Joan Crawford in *They All Kissed the Bride*, 1942
Everett Collection

109
The Duke and
Duchess of Windsor
in the Bahamas,
ca. 1940
Everett Collection

much-photographed elegance—and that of the Duke of Windsor (as Edward was titled after stepping down from the throne)—became world famous, and the mannish look of the big shoulder and "spectator" pump, in two boldly contrasting colors, won haute monde acceptance (Figs. 109–11).

In film, perhaps no example better illustrates the power of shoes than the 1942 classic *Now, Voyager* starring Bette Davis as an ugly-duckling socialite turned swan. Tellingly, the camera's first close-up of her metamorphosis—while on a cruise to South America—shows her exquisite spectator pumps, and glides up to her perfect tailoring and then to her profile, framed by her broad-brimmed hat. The shot epitomizes the transformative power of dress, and the star's starkly beautiful two-tone shoes clearly speak the language of fashion. In the same year that the film was released, *Life* magazine carried an advertisement for a lookalike shoe, demonstrating how sensitive Hollywood was to footwear and fashion bestsellers; the nearly identical shoe in the Weitzman Collection recalls this iconic moment in film history (Figs. 112–15).

110
Peep-toe spectator
pump, ca. 1942
Suede, leather
Stuart Weitzman
Collection, no. 102

111
**Spectator pumps
signed by the
Yankees**, ca. 1936
Leather
Stuart Weitzman
Collection, no. 286

During Joe DiMaggio's
rookie year with the
Yankees, he had his
teammates sign a
pair of his girlfriend's
shoes. Twenty-seven
players (eighteen of
them future winners
of the 1941 World
Series) autographed
this otherwise ordinary
pair of pumps.

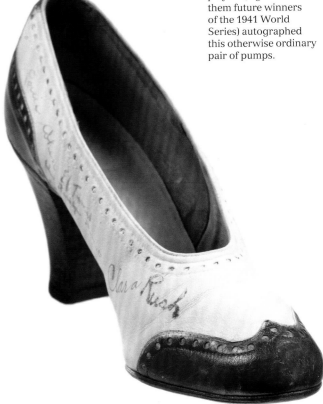

Spectators

All the newest members of this smart young family . . ready to go places, in the typical American way

$7.95 quality features . . . pretty lizard trim

$4.98 Pair

3 widths in our Very Best Spectator . . . representing Very Best materials and skilled workmanship (found only in highest-priced shoes). Uppers of finest grade white suede leather (selected for softness, smoothness, smartness). And the clever trim is lizard—real lizard—with that truly expensive "quality" look . . . with those height-of-style airs. Elasticized—made stretchable with genuine "Lastex" yarn for glove-like fit. Select grade leather sole flexes to finger touch, yet gives the restful support you need. Comfort-height, easy-going 2-inch heel. The most for your money . . . in fashion and quality.

Sizes 6, 6½, 7, 7½, 8, 8½, 9, 9½, 10 in AAA width.   Sizes 5, 5½, 6, 6½, 7, 7½, 8, 8½, 9, 9½, 10 in AA width.   Sizes 4, 4½, 5, 5½, 6, 6½, 7, 7½, 8, 8½, 9, 9½, 10 in A width.   Sizes 4, 4½, 5, 5½, 6, 6½, 7, 7½, 8, 8½, 9, 9½, 10 in C width.   State size and width.   Shipping weight, 1 pound 2 ounces.

◆ 5 L 8610—White with tan genuine lizard trim
◆ 5 L 8613—White with blue genuine lizard trim.   Pair....................$4.98

Classic Pump or Tie . . . 3 heels . . . 2 trims

$2.19 Pair

Note that the pump can be had trimmed in blue, too. Wear 'em for daytime or date-time . . . White Nubuck leather uppers (in both Pump and Oxford styles) trimmed to "belittle" your foot. Leather sole. 1½-inch, 2-inch or 2⅜-inch Cuban heel.
Sizes 3½, 4, 4½, 5, 5½, 6, 6½, 7, 7½, 8, 8½, 9 in A width.   Sizes 3½, 4, 4½, 5, 5½, 6, 6½, 7, 7½, 8, 8½, 9 in C width. State size, width.
54 L 7168—White Leather Oxford. Tan trim. 2-in. Cuban Heel
54 L 7165—White Leather Pump. Patent trim. 2½-in. Cuban Heel
54 L 7164—White Leather Pump. Tan trim. 2½-in. Cuban Heel
54 L 7298—White Leather Pump. Blue trim. 2½-in. Cuban Heel
Shipping weight, 1 pound 3 ounces.   Pair...............$2.19

Usual $4.00 features . . . alligator-grained trim

$3.49 Pair

Costs more than shoe at left—and no wonder! This pert, pretty Spectator is filled with quality and fashion features you'd expect to find in most expensive shoes. So tiny-looking with its perky bow, smart alligator-grained trim . . . so smooth-fitting because it's made stretchable with genuine "Lastex" yarns . . . so roomy with its walled toe. Choice quality leather uppers (whether you choose slipper-soft white suede or soft beige crushed kid). Select grade leather sole is flexible—conforms with each movement of your foot, gives you 8 a.m. pep at 5 p.m.! Smart-looking . . . easy-walking 2½-inch Cuban heel.
Sizes 6, 6½, 7, 7½, 8, 8½, 9 in AA width.   Sizes 5, 5½, 6, 6½, 7, 7½, 8, 8½, 9 in B width. Sizes 4, 4½, 5, 5½, 6, 6½, 7, 7½, 8, 8½, 9 in C width. State size and width. Shipping weight, 1 pound 2 ounces.
◆ 5 L 8604—Beige Crushed kid. Tan alligator-grained trim.
◆ 5 L 8605—White Suede. Tan alligator-grained trim.   Pair.............$3.49

140 . . SEARS, ROEBUCK AND CO.

◆ Before numbers on these two pages means sent from Chicago. Order and pay postage from Sears nearest Mail Order House.   **EXPLANATION OF WIDTHS** on opposite pages.

That Hollywood was one of America's most powerful cultural forces and lucrative industries had already been proved in the 1930s. Early color television was first introduced to many Americans at the 1939 New York World's Fair. The same year also marked the premieres of 365 feature films, with three of the Academy Award nominees for best film now classed among the top one hundred best in cinema history.[28] *Gone with the Wind* won the Oscar that year, vying with the equally beloved *Wizard of Oz*. Dorothy's celebrated "ruby slippers" transported her to Oz on the Yellow Brick Road as everyone sang, "We're off to see the Wizard, the wonderful Wizard of Oz." Such magical footwear, as potent as Cinderella's glass slipper and folklore's seven-league boots, suggests the mythic power of the right shoes. Then, as now, red shoes radiated allure, and scarlet shoes are standouts in the Weitzman Collection (Fig. 116).

The film industry's wide and varied influences lie behind many exciting styles of the 1950s (Figs. 117–27).

116
Stuart Weitzman,
designer
Diamanté pumps, 1969
Leather, crystals
Stuart Weitzman
Collection, no. 226

117
Stanley Philipson,
designer
**Open-toe slingback
shoes**, ca. 1959
Suede, leather,
rhinestones
Stuart Weitzman
Collection, no. 240

118
T-strap sandals,
ca. 1950
Kid leather
Stuart Weitzman
Collection, no. 236

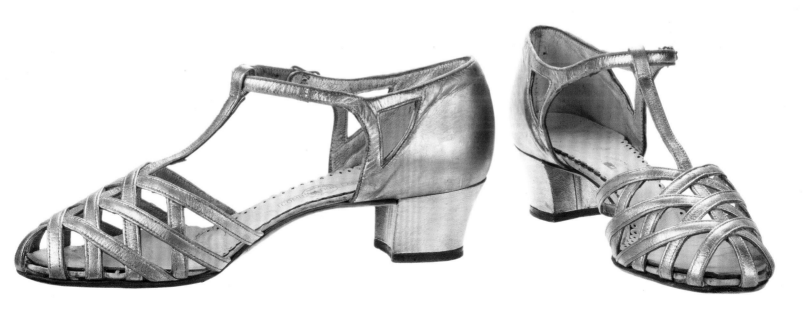

119
Peep-toe mules,
ca. 1950
Kid leather
Stuart Weitzman
Collection, no. 235

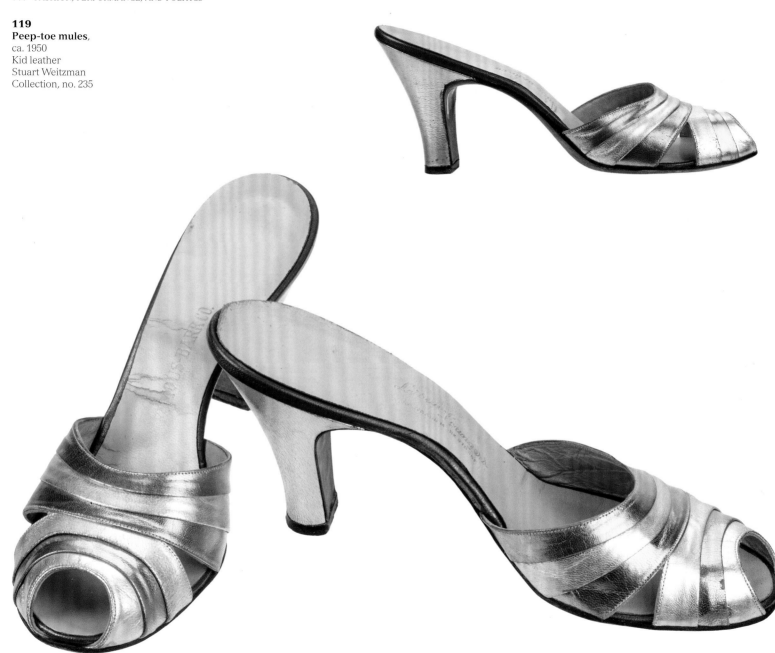

120
Ankle-strap evening shoes, ca. 1953
Leather, rhinestones
Stuart Weitzman
Collection, no. 230

121
Salvatore Ferragamo,
designer
Madonna sandals,
Florence, Italy,
ca. 1954–55
Kid leather, Tavarnelle
needlepoint lace,
embroidery, beads
Stuart Weitzman
Collection, no. 57

122
Stanley Philipson,
designer
**Pointed-toe slingback
evening shoes**,
late 1950s
Vinyl, leather,
rhinestones
Stuart Weitzman
Collection, no. 77

123
Pumps, ca. 1956
Satin, beads, embroidery
Stuart Weitzman
Collection, 127

124
Pumps, Hong Kong,
ca. 1958
Leather, beads,
embroidery
Stuart Weitzman
Collection, no. 150

125
U.S. poster art,
Designing Woman,
1957
Everett Collection

126
Beth Levine, designer
Herbert Levine
Pasha open-toe mules, New York, ca. 1958
Suede, metal, rhinestones
Stuart Weitzman
Collection, no. 252

127
**Peep-toe slingback
shoes**, ca. 1956
Vinyl, leather,
rhinestones
Stuart Weitzman
Collection, no. 248

CONFLICTS, POSTWAR AMERICA, AND CELEBRITY DESIGNERS

With America's entry into World War II in December 1941, U.S. fashion was subjected to government restrictions on its use of materials. To conserve goods, the War Production Board (WPB) made manufacturers responsible for conserving fabrics and especially leather—both essentials for military uniforms and boots. Stanley Marcus (of the Neiman Marcus store) had been appointed to oversee the restrictions on women's dress, introducing slender silhouettes and eliminating ruffles, dolman sleeves, multiple pleats, linings, cuffs, pocket flaps, and anything else extraneous. Rationing limited shoes with leather soles to three pairs per person a year, returning women to the consumption level of the early 1920s.[29] High heels were cut down to more comfortable heights, and, pioneered by the assertive female stars Katharine Hepburn and Marlene Dietrich in the 1930s, pants

were more widely accepted when women, for the first time, took on many predominately male jobs for the war effort and wanted comfort and gender neutrality in their clothing—and as well as the chance to conceal the runs in their now costly silk stockings. The need for safe, comfortable shoes on the factory floor popularized heel-less "flats" and other "sensible" shoes. "Unrationed Shoes" escaped restrictions, however, because they were made without leather. Sold by Lane Bryant and other U.S. retailers, these styles included slingbacks, open-toe styles, and a runaway hit, the wedge shoe. "Wedgies" elevate the wearer on unitary, roughly triangular soles, which are more stable than heels. These were surprisingly comfortable and reasonably priced, and women widely embraced the novel and sporty style[30] (Figs. 128–29). At that time shoe bodies or "uppers" often were made of sturdy cloth or woven fibers; always the innovator, Ferragamo carved sculptural versions and covered them in varied hues of suede and other fabrics, and plaited or crocheted the uppers in raffia, hemp, and even cellophane.

128
Cover, *Vogue*, May 1,
1941
John Rawlings / Vogue
© Condé Nast
Courtesy of the New
York Public Library

129
**Platform wedge
sandals**, ca. 1950
Leather, cork
Stuart Weitzman
Collection, no. 275

High-fashion options also became heftier, and the designs could be quite innovative and amusing. The platform shoe, which raises both the foot and the heel, reached a dazzling variety of heights, and was popularized by film stars and fashionistas. By 1940, Dietrich was standing tall on platform shoes, while the Brazilian actress and samba queen Carmen Miranda made them famous by using them in her signature costumes, along with towering, fruit-laden turbans. This style also helped her gain height: she was all of five feet tall (Figs. 130–31).

130
Carmen Miranda
returning on the
SS *America* **to New**
York from Europe,
1948
Everett Collection

131
Carmen Miranda
modeling platform
shoes, 1944
Bettmann / Getty
Images

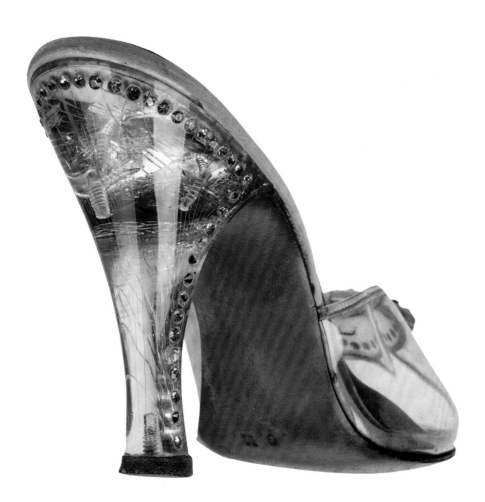

Postwar America enjoyed economic expansion, redirection of wartime production to booming middle-class consumption, and an unbounded belief in a great future. In contrast to the utilitarian designs of the wartime period, footwear reflected new, supremely feminine styles, signaling the collective cultural pressure for women to leave the workforce and return to their prewar "place" in the home.

Since the 1920s the American public had been accustomed to associating company names with mass-market footwear, but after World War II department stores began to promote shoes identified by their designer, stressing their uniqueness and innovation. One notable example was introduced in 1953 by designer Beth Levine, wife and business partner of U.S. shoe manufacturer Herbert Levine. She adopted an elastic device called the "Spring-o-Lator" that supported the instep and kept a backless shoe in place. Her first pair of shoes with the device was dubbed "Ballin' the Jack," and she paid the patentee Maxwell Sachs five cents per pair for its use.[31] The Spring-o-Lator features in several examples in the Weitzman Collection (Figs.132–33, 135–36). The celebrated dancer Ginger Rogers, who had long faced the challenge of dancing in heels (Fig. 134), found this innovation effective. Levine's colorful and exuberant designs had great success in appealing to young, trendy consumers, especially her thigh-high fashion boots that complimented the shrinking hemlines of the 1960s (see Fig. 153, p. 183). Her success led New York's Saks Fifth Avenue

132
Open-toe mules,
ca. 1950s
Leather, plexiglass,
rhinestone, elastic
Spring-o-Lator
Stuart Weitzman
Collection, no. 155

133
Peep-toe mules,
mid-1950s
Plastic, Lucite, leather,
elastic Spring-o-Lator
Stuart Weitzman
Collection, no. 84

134
**Fred Astaire and
Ginger Rogers in**
Follow the Fleet, 1936
Everett Collection

135
Beth Levine, designer
Herbert Levine
**Shining Hour evening
mules**, ca. 1953
Silk, rhinestones, elastic
Spring-o-Lator
Stuart Weitzman
Collection, no. 51

136
Open-toe mules,
ca. 1955
Leather, plastic,
rhinestones, elastic
Spring-o-Lator
Stuart Weitzman
Collection, no. 92

to establish within its shoe department a boutique named Beth's Bootery.[32]

Postwar Hollywood continued to influence footwear and fashion. During the late 1940s and throughout the 1950s, pseudo-historical "sword and sandal" films such as *Samson and Delilah* (1949; Fig. 137) and *The Prodigal* (1955) used casts of thousands to recreate Old Testament stories. Designers were able to dress actresses in thin, revealing costumes, sidestepping enforcers of the puritanical and restrictive Hays Code, on the grounds that such garments were authentically historical.[33] Starring such beauties as Lana Turner and Hedy Lamarr as high priestesses and courtesans, Biblical spectacles inspired bejeweled sandals of gold and silver kid, versions of which soon twinkled on dance floors throughout the country (Fig. 138).

In 1961, when Hubert de Givenchy dressed Audrey Hepburn for *Breakfast at Tiffany's*, he recruited the chic French couturier-turned-footwear-designer Roger Vivier to complete the winsome actress's stylish look. For this romantic film based on Truman Capote's short story, Vivier's simple, pointed-toe pumps set off Givenchy's equally svelte gowns (Figs. 139–40). So influential was Hepburn's iconic look that Stuart Weitzman revived it twenty years later, reinterpreting Vivier's classic pointed toe and low kitten heel in richly textured *peau de soie* satin (Fig. 141).

137
Hedy Lamarr in
Samson and Delilah,
1949
Everett Collection

138
**T-strap evening
sandals**, ca. 1940s
Leather, silk,
rhinestones
Stuart Weitzman
Collection, no. 99

139
Publicity still,
Breakfast at Tiffany's,
1961
Everett Collection

140
Poster art, *Breakfast at Tiffany's,* 1961
Everett Collection

141
Stuart Weitzman, designer
Kitten-heel pumps,
ca. 1980s
Peau de soie
Stuart Weitzman Collection, no. 287

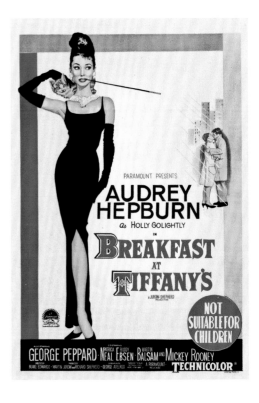

POP AND POPULAR STYLES IN THE 1960s

A Wharton Business School graduate, the young Weitzman apprenticed in his father's shoe manufacturing business, Mr. Seymour, or Seymour Shoes, learning the craft as well as the artistry of shoe design.[34] During the 1964 New York World's Fair, the younger Weitzman took over the company.[35] This launched a career extending the family tradition of producing elegant and inventive quality footwear, and the tools and machinery used assured that the stitch count of his factory-made footwear matched that of bespoke shoemaking. Mr. Seymour shoes were both elegant and topical, referencing the aesthetics and cultural preoccupations of the day. With their open sides and extreme pointed toes (see, e.g., Figs. 142–44), the shoes are sleek and almost futuristic, reflecting the 1960s fascination with the space race to the moon.

142
Seymour Weitzman,
designer
Mr. Seymour
**Pointed-toe laced
pumps**, ca. 1964
Suede, grosgrain ribbon
Stuart Weitzman
Collection, no. 269

143
Seymour Weitzman,
designer
Mr. Seymour
Pointed-toe pumps,
ca. 1964
Leather, rhinestones
Stuart Weitzman
Collection, no. 270

144 [below]
Seymour Weitzman,
designer
Mr. Seymour
**Pointed-toe slingback
shoes**, ca. 1964
Leather, net
Stuart Weitzman
Collection, no. 271

145 [opposite]
**Mary Quant (front,
center) at a show of
her footwear range,
Quant Afoot**,
1967
Alamy

"Make Love Not War" and "Flower Power" were among the early slogans of the late 1960s and the early 1970s movements centered around protesting the Vietnam War, promoting the relaxing of sexual and cultural mores, and an ebullient social and cultural upheaval. This was also an effervescent period for design, energized by youth and political and social rebellions. Flowers ornamented walls, cars, vans, and clothes. Fashion looks confected of painted, printed, tie-dyed, and embroidered vests, bell-bottom pants, and floppy hats turned some big-city public spaces into a garden of walking blossoms. Carnaby Street in London, electrified by designers such as Mary Quant and Ossie Clark, was the center of this anti-mainstream fashion that became a fashion in itself (Fig. 145). Platform heels were back in fashion (Fig. 146), and it is no surprise that an open-toed pair of "Flower Power" platform heels, stamped "Chelsea Cobbler 33 Sackville WI" features lifelike Tudor roses on the instep in dark red suede (Fig. 147).

146
John Elari
People, Parks
Central Park, New York,
1972
Kodachrome slide
New-York Historical
Society Library

147
**Peep-toe platform
shoes**, ca. 1972
Suede
Stuart Weitzman
Collection, no. 258

Although it is unclear who actually invented the modern miniskirt (a tribute to 1920s chemise dresses, but with even higher hems), the style was extremely popular in the 1960s, particularly in London. Mods and rockers created such short skirts that those of us who were living in London at the time and wore them believed that bell-bottoms were the hippies' reassertion of modesty. Setting off knees and legs (now smoothed in pantyhose or fish-net stockings), "go-go" boots—emblematic of the Youthquake's love of fad dancing—climbed thigh-high and flaunted ornaments, fringes, and cutouts evoking outré styles from cowboy gear to science-fiction film costumes. Paris and London competed with American designers who used Lurex and other metallics as well as form-revealing "stretch fibers" for garments, while vinyl and similar synthetics served "nude" or neon-hued footwear (Figs. 148–52). Psychedelic patterns and Day-Glo colors dazzled dancers and fans at rock concerts where light shows pulsed to the beat. Young people expressed their radical politics with marches and sit-ins, but also with "sex, drugs, and rock 'n' roll," the mantra for the period's more openly available pastimes. The new fashions also signaled a new era for women, as feminism and reproductive options initiated by the Pill reflected a new sense of female empowerment.

148
Arsho Baghsarian,
designer
Design for I. Miller,
ca. 1963–68
Graphite and colored
pencil on vellum
Courtesy of Fashion
Institute of Technology
| SUNY, Gladys Marcus
Library Department of
Special Collections

149
Thong sandals, 1960s
Leather, synthetic
Stuart Weitzman
Collection, no. 238

150
Square-toe shoes,
ca. 1970
Vinyl, plexiglass,
kid leather
Stuart Weitzman
Collection, no. 100

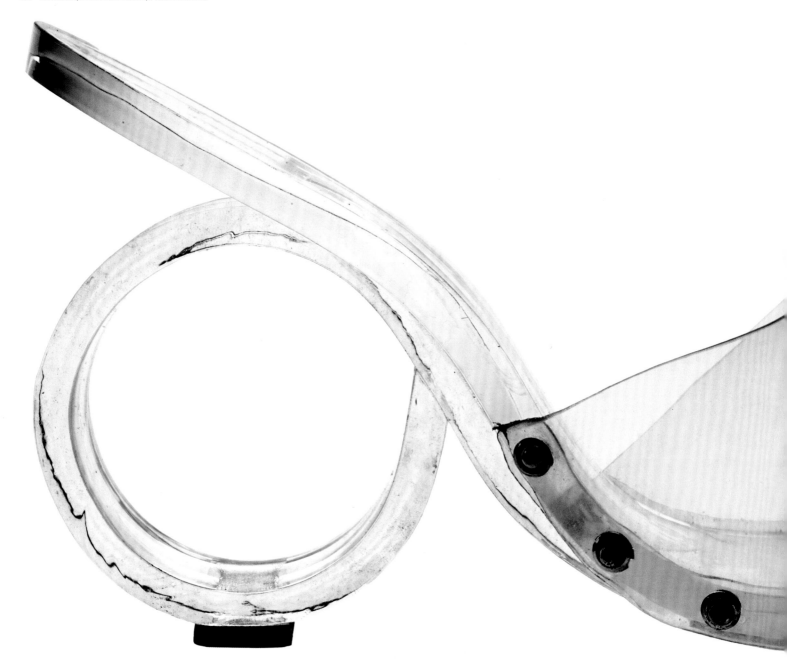

151
Open-toe mule,
ca. 1965
Lucite, vinyl, metal
screws and grommets
Stuart Weitzman
Collection, no. 242

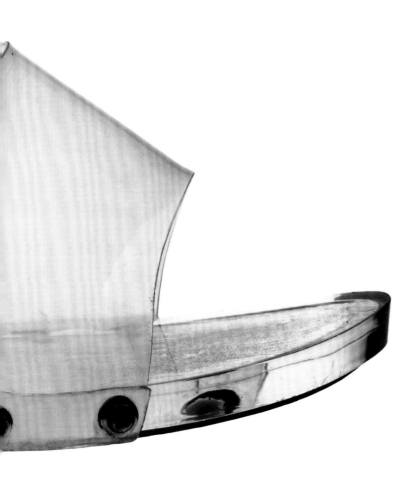

152
Beth Levine, designer
Herbert Levine
Pumps, ca. 1960
Vinyl, kid leather, Lucite
Stuart Weitzman
Collection, no. 243

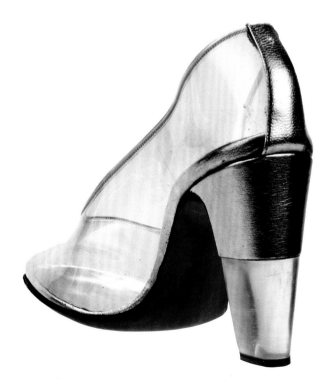

In 1966, Nancy Sinatra released a catchy soundtrack for the times with her number one hit, "These Boots are Made for Walkin'," flaunting a white pair of Beth Levine boots in publicity photos (Fig. 153).[36]

Shoes of the 1960s can reflect the energy of feminist empowerment or express pop themes in up-market elegance (Figs. 154–59).

153
Nancy Sinatra, 1968
Starstock / Photoshot /
Courtesy of the Everett
Collection

154
**Peep-toe slingback
shoes**, ca. 1967
Leather, satin
Stuart Weitzman
Collection, no. 246

155
Pointed-toe pumps,
ca. 1965
Mille fleur leather
Stuart Weitzman
Collection, no. 209

156
Square-toe low-heel
shoes, ca. 1960
Leather, beads
Stuart Weitzman
Collection, no. 202

157
Bridal shoes, 1967
Satin, beads
Stuart Weitzman
Collection, no. 183

158
Beth Levine, designer
Herbert Levine
**Kabuki platform
shoes**, 1964
Suede, wood
Stuart Weitzman
Collection, no. 68

159
Pointed-toe mules,
ca. 1966
Satin
Stuart Weitzman
Collection, no. 131

THE TURN-OF-THE-CENTURY STANCE

In the mid-1970s and throughout the 1980s, sheer spectacles generated by Hollywood, Broadway, London's West End, and the music industry largely dominated popular culture, and an expanded mass-market press led by *People* magazine relentlessly pursued their stars. Entertainers and aristocrats again shared meticulous media attention, and what was worn by Elton John, KISS, ABBA, Patti LaBelle, the Sex Pistols, and Michael Jackson on tour or on TV was reported alongside details about Princess Diana's hats and First Lady Nancy Reagan's size 2 gowns. Shoes were no longer simply dyed to match, and fun and fantasy were no longer restricted to women's footwear. Shoes for all genders and genres, from sneakers to platforms, and disco sandals to Doc Martens, became part of the fashion parade.

Into the 1990s, Stuart Weitzman's own designs reflected, among other things, an interest in revival styles. His ankle boot (Fig. 160) recalls a high-buttoned boot of 1918 (see Fig. 30, p. 53), exemplifying the evergreen attraction of retro fashion history in the industry. His Cinderella sandals update fairy-tale glamour with Plexiglas, Swarovski crystals, and super-high heels (Fig. 165). By the turn of the century, "ravers" revived funk and disco styles, and bands like the Spice Girls ushered in "third wave" feminism and the concept of "girl power," embodied in outrageously tall shoes and some of fashion history's most astonishing footwear to date. Alongside classics in traditional leather and suede appeared reinterpretations in vinyl and plastics (Figs. 161–64). While fashion footwear has always held a prominent place in any good wardrobe, not to mention the erotic imagination, the turn of the century saw the fetishizing of footwear like never before. This was demonstrated nowhere better than the central role of the high-heeled shoe in the TV series *Sex and the City*.

The new millennium has already demonstrated new directions for footwear, influenced by contemporary innovations and preoccupations, not the least being new technologies, concern for the environment, and growing acceptance of gender fluidity. Where future footwear fashions will go remains to be seen, as newer generations face novel challenges and embrace different ideologies and aesthetics. Whatever those may be, Stuart Weitzman will be walking beside them, creating beautifully crafted, aesthetically delightful and culturally relevant shoes to reflect emerging tastes, and—no doubt—adding to his fascinating historic collection.

160
Stuart Weitzman, designer
Ankle boots, 1986
Leather, elastic, buttons
Stuart Weitzman Collection, no. 21

Worn by the cast of Andrew Lloyd Webber's *Phantom of the Opera*

195

161
Terry de Havilland,
designer
**Peep-toe platform
shoes**, ca. 1972
Suede, leather
Stuart Weitzman
Collection, no. 257

162
**Glass Slipper open-
toe slingback shoes**,
early 1970s
Vinyl, leather, Lucite
Stuart Weitzman
Collection, no. 115

163
Stuart Weitzman,
designer
**Open-toe ankle-strap
evening shoes**, ca. 1972
Leather, sequins, beads
Stuart Weitzman
Collection, no. 54

164
David Evins, designer
Column-heel pumps,
ca. 1970
Plastic
Stuart Weitzman
Collection, no. 81

165
Stuart Weitzman,
designer
Cinderella sandals,
ca. 1998
Vinyl, Plexiglas,
Swarovski crystals
Stuart Weitzman
Collection, no. 288

Minnie Driver wore
these sandals to
the Oscars in 1998,
the year she was
nominated for the Best
Supporting Actress
award for her role in
Good Will Hunting.

NOTES

STANDING IN HEELS, STANDING ON PRINCIPLE? Valerie Paley

1 "Ask Them Yourself: Question for Bette Midler," *Herald Statesman* (Yonkers, NY), January 13, 1980, Family Weekly Newspaper supplement.

2 Helen Persson, ed., *Shoes: Pleasure and Pain*, (London: Victoria and Albert Museum, 2015), 47.

3 Jenna Sauers, "Wearing Heels Does Not Make You a Bad Feminist," *Jezebel*, March 22, 2012, http://jezebel.com/5895613/wearing-heels-does-not-make-you-a-bad-feminist.

4 Marylin Bender, "What's in a Shoe Name? Mainly Confusion, Shoppers Discover," *New York Times*, April 13, 1964.

5 Pamela G. Hollie, "Shoe Industry's Struggle," *New York Times*, May 28, 1985.

6 Euromonitor International, *Footwear in the US*, Market Research Report, February 2017, http://www.euromonitor.com/footwear-in-the-us/report. Sports footwear, and styles that "complement an active lifestyle," represent 41 percent of 2016 total sales.

7 Eric Wilson, "Beth Levine, 'First Lady of Shoe Design,' Is Dead at 91," *New York Times*, September 23, 2006.

8 Anne-Marie Schiro, "Herbert Levine, 75, Manufacturer of High-Fashion Women's Shoes," *New York Times*, August 10, 1991.

9 Frederick Allen, *The Shoe Industry* (Boston: Vocation Bureau of Boston, 1916), 262, 290.

10 Ava F. Kahn, "Mary Ann Cohen Magnin," *Jewish Women: A Comprehensive Historical Encyclopedia*, Jewish Women's Archive, March 1, 2009, https://jwa.org/encyclopedia/article/magnin-mary-ann-cohen.

11 News Desk, "Arresting Dress: A Timeline of Anti-Cross-Dressing Laws in the United States," *PBS Newshour*, May 31, 2015, http://www.pbs.org/newshour/updates/arresting-dress-timeline-anti-cross-dressing-laws-u-s.

12 Angela Taylor, "The 4-Inch Heel Returns—But This Time, It's for Men," *New York Times*, February 19, 1972.

FASHION, PERFORMANCE, AND POLITICS: An Introduction to the Stuart Weitzman Collection Edward Maeder

1 I argue this point at more length in "Decent Exposure: Status, Excess, the World of Couturier," in *Seductive Surfaces: The Art of Tissot*, Studies in British Art 6, ed. Katharine Lochnan (New Haven and London: Yale University Press, 1999), 75.

2 Stella Mary Newton, OBE, "Fashions in Fashion History," *Times Literary Supplement* (London), March 21, 1975, 305.

3 Caroline Cox, *Vintage Shoes: Collecting and Wearing Twentieth-Century Designer Footwear* (New York: Collins Design, 2008), 8.

4 Bernard Rudofsky, *Are Clothes Modern? An Essay on Contemporary Apparel* (Chicago: Paul Theobald, 1947), 38. This book originated with an exhibition at New York's Museum of Modern Art in 1944–45.

5 Mrs. Frances Milton Trollope, *Domestic Manners of the Americans* (1832), quoted in Nancy E. Rexford, *Women's Shoes in America, 1795–1930* (Kent, OH, and London: Kent State University Press, 2000), 38.

6 Fully discussed in Elizabeth Semmelhack, *Standing Tall: The Curious History of Men in Heels* (Toronto, Ontario, Canada: Bata Shoe Museum Foundation, 2015). Semmelhack's history of the evolution of men's heels from "power signifier" to today's "gender disruptor" accompanied an exhibition of the same name at the Bata Shoe Museum, Toronto, in 2015–16.

7 Colin McDowell, *Shoes: Fashion and Fantasy* (New York: Rizzoli, 1989), 28.

8 Ibid., 12.

9 Aileen Ribeiro, *The Dress Worn at Masquerades in England, 1730–1790, and Its Relation to Fancy Dress in Portraiture*, Outstanding Theses from the Courtauld Institute of Art (New York and London: Garland, 1984), 236.

10 McDowell, *Shoes*, 14.

11 H. R. Haweis, *The Art of Beauty*, 2nd ed. (London: Chatto & Windus, 1883), 93.

12 Rexford, *Women's Shoes in America*, 4–5.

13 Ibid., 9, 19–20.

14 Frederick Lewis Allen, *The Big Change: America Transforms Itself, 1900–1950* (New York: Bantam Books, 1965), 99.

15 William A. Rossi, "How American Fashion Was Born," *Footwear News* (Fairchild Publications, New York), March 22, 1999, 30.

16 Ibid.

17 Rexford, *Women's Shoes in America*, 25–29.

18 Ibid.

19 Rossi, "How American Fashion Was Born," 30.

20 Rexford, *Women's Shoes in America*, 28.

21 *Star-Gazette* (Elmira, New York), April 16, 1912, 4.

22 Loretta Carrillo, "Dance," in *Handbook of American Popular Culture*, 2nd ed., ed. M. Thomas Inge (New York; Westport, CT; and London: Greenwood Press, 1989), 262.

23 Ibid., 263.

24 "Car Again Chosen Officially to Lead Dancers," "Dance from Los Angeles to Ocean Beach [Santa Monica]," *Los Angeles Times*, April 8, 1928, 106.

25 Author's interview with historian and author Satch LaValley on April 18, 1986, in preparation for the publication *Hollywood and History: Costume Design in Film* (London and New York: Thames & Hudson; Los Angeles: Los Angeles County Museum of Art, 1987), catalogue for the exhibition of the same name, Los Angeles County Museum of Art, California, 1987–88.

26 Salvatore Ferragamo, *Shoemaker of Dreams: The Autobiography of Salvatore Ferragamo* (New York: Crown Publishers, 1972), 89.

27 Elsa Schiaparelli, *Shocking Life* (New York: E. P. Dutton, 1954), 76 (shoulders), 114 (hat; a collaboration with Dalí).

28 Tom Flannery, *1939, The Year in Movies: A Comprehensive Filmography* (Jefferson, NC, and London: McFarland, 1990), xiii. For the Oscar nominees of 1939 in a respected "best film" list, see American Film Institute, "AFI's 100 Years . . . 100 Movies," June 16, 1998, http://www.afi.com/100Years/movies.aspx.

29 Rossi, "How American Fashion Was Born," 30.

30 Victoria and Albert Museum, *A History of Shoes* (London: Victoria and Albert Museum, 2015), http://www.vam.ac.uk/shoestimeline. This interactive timeline originated with the 2015 V&A exhibition "Shoes: Pleasure and Pain"; utilitarian designs, it notes, were introduced by the government in 1941 to counter rising clothing costs.

31 Maxwell Sachs of Boston was a shoe manufacturer: Helene Verin, *Beth Levine Shoes* (New York: Stewart, Tabori & Chang, 2009), 35.

32 Ibid., 45.

33 Author's conversation with film costume designer Walter Plunkett (*Gone With the Wind*) in June 1979 at the Los Angeles Country Museum of Art.

34 Stuart Weitzman interviewed by Barbara Bradley for "Mules, Naked Sandals Will Be the Rage in the New Millennium," *Fond du Lac Commonwealth Reporter* (Fond du Lac, Wisconsin), September 2, 1999, 17.

35 Seymour Weitzman died on September 8: Obituary, *New York Times*, September 10, 1965, 32.

36 Helene Verin, *Beth Levine Shoes* (New York: Stewart, Tabori & Chang, 2009), 45.

BIBLIOGRAPHY

Abbott, Edith. "Women in Industry: The Manufacture of Boots and Shoes." *American Journal of Sociology* 15, no. 3 (1909): 335–60.

Allen, Frederick J. *The Shoe Industry*. Boston: Vocation Bureau of Boston, 1916.

Allen, Frederick Lewis. *The Big Change: America Transforms Itself, 1900–1950*. New York: Bantam Books, 1965.

Benson, Susan Porter. *Counter Cultures: Saleswomen, Managers, and Customers in American Department Stores, 1890–1940*. Chicago: University of Illinois Press, 1988.

Carrillo, Loretta. "Dance." In *Handbook of American Popular Culture*, 2nd ed. Edited by M. Thomas Inge. New York: Greenwood Press 1989.

Cox, Caroline. *Vintage Shoes: Collecting and Wearing Twentieth-Century Designer Footwear*. New York: Collins Design, 2008.

Enstad, Nan. *Ladies of Labor, Girls of Adventure: Working Women, Popular Culture, and Labor Politics at the Turn of the Twentieth Century*. New York: Columbia University Press, 1999.

Erenberg, Lewis A. *Steppin' Out: New York Nightlife and the Transformation of American Culture, 1890–1930*. Chicago: University of Chicago Press, 1981.

Euromonitor International. *Footwear in the US*. Market research report. Chicago: Euromonitor International, February 2017. http://www.euromonitor.com/footwear-in-the-us/report.

Ferragamo, Salvatore. *Shoemaker of Dreams: The Autobiography of Salvatore Ferragamo*. New York: Crown, 1972.

Flannery, Tom. *1939, The Year in Movies: A Comprehensive Filmography*. Jefferson, NC, and London: McFarland, 1990.

Kahn, Ava F. "Mary Ann Cohen Magnin, 1849–1943." *Jewish Women: A Comprehensive Historical Encyclopedia*. Jewish Women's Archive. March 1, 2009. https://jwa.org/encyclopedia/article/magnin-mary-ann-cohen.

Haweis, H. R. *The Art of Beauty*, 2nd ed. London: Chatto & Windus, 1883.

Leach, William. *Land of Desire: Merchants, Power, and the Rise of a New American Culture*. New York: Vintage Books, 1993.

Maeder, Edward. "Decent Exposure: Status, Excess, the World of Couturier." In *Seductive Surfaces: The Art of Tissot*. Studies in British Art 6. Edited by Katharine Lochnan. New Haven and London: Yale University Press, 1999.

Maeder, Edward. *Hollywood and History: Costume Design in Film*. Exhibition catalogue. New York: Thames and Hudson; Los Angeles: Los Angeles County Museum of Art, 1987.

McDowell, Colin. *Shoes: Fashion and Fantasy*. New York: Rizzoli, 1989.

McMains, Juliet. *Glamor Addiction: Inside the American Ballroom Dance Industry*. Middletown, CT: Wesleyan University Press, 2006.

Mendes, Valerie, Stefania Ricci, and Deborah Hodges. *Salvatore Ferragamo: The Art of the Shoe, 1927–1960*. Florence, Italy: Centro Di, 1987.

News Desk. "Arresting Dress: A Timeline of Anti-Cross-Dressing Laws in the United States." *PBS Newshour*, May 31, 2015. http://www.pbs.org/newshour/updates/arresting-dress-timeline-anti-cross-dressing-laws-u-s.

Nystron, Paul H. *The Economics of Fashion*. New York: The Ronald Press Company, 1928.

Persson, Helen, ed. *Shoes: Pleasure and Pain*. London: Victoria and Albert Museum, 2015.

Rexford, Nancy. *Women's Shoes in America, 1795–1930*. Kent, OH, and London: Kent State University Press, 2000.

Ribeiro, Aileen. *The Dress Worn at Masquerades in England, 1730–1790, and Its Relation to Fancy Dress in Portraiture*. Outstanding Theses from the Courtauld Institute of Art. New York and London: Garland, 1984.

Rudofsky, Bernard. *Are Clothes Modern? An Essay on Contemporary Apparel*. Chicago: Paul Theobald, 1947.

Schiaparelli, Elsa. *Shocking Life*. New York: E. P. Dutton, 1954.

Semmelhack, Elizabeth. *Heights of Fashion: A History of the Elevated Shoe*. Periscope Publishing/ The Bata Shoe Museum – Pittsburgh, PA/ Toronto, Ontario 2008.

Semmelhack, Elizabeth. *Standing Tall: The Curious History of Men in Heels*. Exhibition catalogue. Toronto, Ontario, Canada: Bata Shoe Museum Foundation, 2015.

Small, Lisa, ed. *Killer Heels: The Art of the High-Heeled Shoe*. New York: Brooklyn Museum and DelMonico Books, 2014.

Steele, Valerie. *Fetish: Fashion, Sex and Power*. New York: Oxford University Press, 1996.

Steele, Valerie. *Shoe Obsession*. New Haven: Yale University Press, 2013.

Thornton, Peter. *Authentic Décor: The Domestic Interior 1620–1920*. London: Weidenfeld & Nicolson, 1984.

Verin, Helene. *Beth Levine Shoes*. New York: Stewart, Tabori & Chang, 2009.

Walford, Jonathan. *The Seductive Shoe: Four Centuries of Fashion Footwear*. New York: Stewart, Tabori & Chang, 2007.

Walford, Jonathan. *Shoes A–Z: Designers, Brands, Manufacturers and Retailers*. Thames & Hudson, 2010.

Young, William H.; Young, Nancy K. *The 1930s*. American Popular Culture Through History. Series editor Ray B. Browne. Westport, CT, and London: Greenwood Press, 2002.

INDEX